Praise for
Every Day Simple

Humble, honest, encouraging, open, and most of all displays God's love for us all.

TERRIE D., 56, DAUGHTER, WIFE, MOTHER,
GRANDMOTHER, FRIEND, ACCOUNTING CLERK

I want to read more!

AMBER M., 38, OFFICE MANAGER

Easy to read, very engaging, and relatable. I love it!

GENIE K., 57, TRANSFORMATIONAL LIFE COACH

I found this book to be so relatable, but also wished I would have had these wise words as a young woman starting married life!

JULIE O., 63, RETIRED

This is an invitation toward simplicity we need in a far too complicated world.

BREKKA, 25, TEACHER

Like a conversation with a good friend or even a grandmother, Every Day Simple *shares hope that comes from problems conquered and lessons learned.*

MARYANN, 36, STAY-AT-HOME-MOM

every day SIMPLE

Living a life of HOPE in a complicated world

Sue L Hamilton

Sue Hamilton

Keep it Simple
+
PRAY

LIVE4ONE ENTERPRISE LLC
Minot, ND

EVERY DAY SIMPLE

Copyright © 2021 Sue L. Hamilton
Live4One Enterprise LLC
P.O. Box 1425
Minot, ND 58702
www.live4oneenterprise.com

Book Design by TLC Book Design, *TLCBookDesign.com*
Cover: Tamara Dever; Interior: Erin Stark

ISBN: 978-0-9993634-3-0 (paperback)   978-0-9993634-4-7 (e-book)

Library of Congress Control Number: 2020924307

Printed in the United States of America

Contents

Prologue

Flying down the Interstate on my back after being thrown from my motorcycle, I believed my life was over, yet, God had other plans. God got the angels' attention with a loud whistle and said, "Go down and get her. Save her from all the bumps, bruises, and broken bones. I have plans for her." And on the command, I was swooped up in the arms of a heavenly angel and gently placed on the shoulder of the road. Landing in a standing position with my eyes peering at the ground.

I was looking at the ground, and as I raised my face—the view was the ditch and houses off in a distance. I was thinking, "Heaven sure looks like Sturgis." Then I realized I wasn't dead! I was ALIVE! But, surely I must be hurt after that crazy ride. To my surprise I had no serious injuries, only a small tear in my jeans on the knee area of my right leg and slight road rash on my left arm which was barely bleeding.

God and angels, am I crazy?

No. I'm a Miracle.

For he will command his angels concerning you to guard you in all your ways; they will lift you up in their hands, so that you will not strike your foot against a stone.

PSALM 91:11-12 NIV

I escaped the life-threatening motorcycle accident with absolutely nothing wrong with me. The motorcycle was in the same shape as me with little damage, and within a few hours I was able to ride away from the accident. The details of the story stay fresh in my mind like they happened yesterday. It was the most scary and terrifying event that has ever happened to me. As I left the scene riding my motorcycle, a question lingered: "Why God? Why did you save ME?" The question may never be fully answered until I stand in front of God. Until then, I believe the Motorcycle Miracle was God's way of getting my attention to truly believe in Him.

A bit of the story for you is this…it was 1996 and I had been clean and sober from alcohol and drugs for six years and had finally removed the cotton from my ears to hear others explain who God was to them. I was beginning to believe there was a God but that my destructive, dark past was still too unforgivable to have Him be part of my life. I would simply have to be satisfied with the realization that I did believe He existed and that I would go to heaven because I know I believed. I didn't believe my life would get much better nor would God ever become more real to me. It was as good as it was going to be.

During this time of questioning if God really was the God others talked about, who was as real as a human to some of them, and who gives them joy each day as He comes alive in their lives, I could not believe my life could be any more than it was at that time. Yet, God has interesting ways of getting our attention, and the accident was my wake-up call.

If you are interested in the remaining details of the motorcycle story and more of my life in addiction to alcohol and drugs, you can read it in my memoir *Carried by Faith: From Substance Abuse to a Life Filled with Miracles.*

When *Carried by Faith* was published, it was a huge accomplishment and a check mark off my bucket list. The book reviews came rolling in with more compliments and expressions of thanks for having the courage to write about a subject that needs to be shared. In addition, many readers would say, "I want to know what happened in your life after the accident." My thoughts were, "That's nice, but I barely completed this book and it took me seven years. I don't know how I would sum up the 'rest of the story.'"

Even after writing two books, *Carried by Faith* and *Journey of Trust*, I still don't feel one hundred percent comfortable saying I'm an author. I will never fit into the traditional ideals of what the world says an author and speaker is to be. The way I communicate is through life stories, analogies, and a tell-it-like-it-is approach with no fluff. God made me the way He did so I can communicate to others He wants to speak to in that same manner. I share my life experiences because of what God has done in and through me. I share the hope that is in God which He has allowed me to experience in a life that is uniquely mine, yet others can relate.

God gave me the gift to ENCOURAGE others. I don't try to convince you to change, I just lay out what has happened to me, that most likely has happened in your life too, and how I let God be the guide in every area of life to show me where He wants me to go. It's this "telling the story" in a simple, basic, and authentic way that expresses God's compassion, love, and hope for each of us that entices others to want to make changes for themselves, opening their minds to become ALL GOD intended them to be.

The books I have written show God's compassion, His hope put into words to communicate what He wants others to know, and how we can draw near to Him. It's humbling to be allowed to be a mouthpiece, formed in the unique way God made me, to share, give hope, and communicate His message.

Introduction

The primary focus of this book is to share how to live every day of our lives with hope with a simple approach in this complicated world. Every day can be a struggle to stay focused on the simple, everyday tasks in our personal world. Wrestling mentally with the what and how to do things that should be easy yet are seemingly complicated. Analyzing things until there are no more viewpoints to review, and only then surrendering in utter defeat to the simplest way to accomplish whatever is in front of us.

This way of thinking has never been easy for me, as I tend to complicate most every situation. I love to run the show, to be in control, spending hours thinking of what needs to be done in the day, how they will be completed, and what the results will be. I've got the plan and it will work out just as I say...1, 2, 3. To think differently takes effort and it does not come easy to me. I work on it daily as I need God to help direct my day; He is the Director, NOT me. It comes down to trusting and believing God can and will do for me what I cannot do for myself.

Many of you can relate to this way of thinking. We are complex, complicated, and try to run the show. Most of us would say we are anything BUT simple, especially EVERY DAY! As we grow older, we come to realize a simple life is what we desire. When we get distracted, we need to redirect our thoughts to God to have Him be our leader on where we are to go for the day. When this simple direction happens, our life is fulfilling and enriched with blessings we can only dream of. Each of us deserves to enjoy days of everyday simplicity in our journey of life so we can see that simple can be beautiful.

Every Day Simple: Living a Life of HOPE in a Complicated World came after the nonstop bashing in my mind of complicating the entire process of what I should write as a follow-up to *Carried by Faith.* God provided all the chapter focuses in an afternoon as I struggled with life and the direction to go. Of course, I was in the driver's seat making my plans and directing where we were going next when God said, "Keep it Simple." Me? I can't keep anything simple. I mess things up with a complex and elaborate plan, and the word "simple" disappears in two seconds. As I have struggled to keep this simple focus for the book, it has spoken to me. I hope it speaks to you too.

Hope

Often I have explained my life as compared to a jigsaw puzzle with no edge pieces. It has felt undefined for many years. Even after I let God in my life, it has taken many attempts to find the border pieces to create some type of perimeter. I need structure as it gives security and lessens fear. Yet, with every attempt to have structure, things would get out of sorts and I could not find the pieces that fit so neatly together.

When I took control of life, the pieces got out of control as I made everything complicated. It was like someone came into my life, the puzzle, took the edges apart piece-by-piece and swirled them amongst the other pieces. Starting over and over seemed to be my norm. I was good at messing things up and not allowing God to take control and be the Director. I was constantly telling God what I needed without ever being quiet enough to hear His still, small voice to direct my life. Difficulties piled up when I would force my control and I would go crashing into the box of pieces to start all over again.

My life has been anything but simple—far from it! So, why would I be writing a book about living life in a simple manner? It's the lessons God has taught me and the ones I

1

have so furiously fought against that made me stop in my tracks to reevaluate life. When I analyze the complexities I have imposed on myself, I see how difficult I have made life. Again, using the puzzle analogy, my life has been sorted out in color sections, the border pieces nicely set out in place and progress is made in certain areas where you can clearly see the completed work, then—bam—I come in with self-will and turn the table upside down with all the pieces tumbling to the floor. It's a big mess that the Master will once again pick up to sort through.

As with this book, I tried to do it my way—to organize the chapters, write extra words that would sound better to the reader, make sure there was a primary message, a captivating story, along with a call to action in each section. I was thinking in my world and what I thought was best, and then it came crashing down, in a literal sense. I lost the book on a thumb drive at the halfway mark of completion only to be forced to start with an older backup version. I suspect God was not liking my direction and had to let that happen. In the pain of losing many hours of work, I became extremely angry, sad, and hopeless just like I did during the writing of *Carried by Faith*. My self-will is strong and doesn't seem to give up easily, so God has to put poignant obstacles in my way to get my attention. He will make sure it's Him only who will control the message of the book.

This project got back on track once my temper tantrum over losing hours of original material had stopped. God in His kind, loving way gently gave me a vision to focus on as I endeavored to continue to complete this book. I was driving to our lake home crying to God, asking how He could have let this happen to me and then this vision was given to me. It was a defining moment that gave me clarity and a solid sense of direction to continue with the project. In my mind I saw a young girl in her late teens or early twenties with a slim, small body with long, wavy brown hair. I could not see her face; it was more of a silhouette without much details. God revealed that the girl was the one who I was to write this book for and her name was Hope and she is my granddaughter. With tears streaming down my face, I knew the vision was from God because we do not have any grandchildren.

This vision has brought clarity to the project and has allowed me to let go of the struggle when I begin to take control and think I know best. When others read this book, they will form many opinions on the stories, ideas shared, focuses, scriptures, and thoughts. But I am reminded each time I write a sentence that the book is for that one person, my granddaughter, whom I have not met yet, but want to share my life story with and how I lived. I want her to see how I found a God I did not know or understand, who loved me unconditionally, who saved me from the pit of hell to raise me up to share my hope with others. The God I love with all my heart showed me love so that I was able to love myself and others. A God who is my best friend, one I seek out every day to help me live a life that I could not live without Him in it.

I can honestly say that the life I live is one I never even dreamed possible as a young girl. To show, through my changed life, an example of what God can do in any person's life once they surrender. To enjoy whatever He's given me, good, bad, and in between, knowing He is the maker of my life. Thank you, God, for continually amazing me and how You can redirect things in a flash of a thought or a blink of an eye.

So as this book has taken on new meaning, I invite you to come alongside me as I share in different ways how I live a life of hope in focusing on simplicity. The sections will have stories of how I have lived since God so graciously entered my life; others are concepts I've studied that have helped me grow; and some are from material I've taught to other women throughout the years. The flow of the book is non-traditional. It may be considered a book of resources or a question and answer book or a self-improvement book. Whichever way it is taken by the reader, I know it is for Hope, for her to be reminded to live a simple life every day in this complicated world.

To you my sweet granddaughter, I share my heritage of hope to live *Every Day Simple*.

But from everlasting to everlasting the Lord's love is with those who fear him, and his righteousness with their children's children—with those who keep his covenant and remember to obey his precepts.

PSALM 103:17-18 NIV

Simple Questions in Life

When recovery crossed my life path in March of 1990 and I made the decision to stay clean and sober from alcohol and drugs, there were many years to make up for in terms of time lost in learning simple basic life skills. Now I was running toward a simple life, one I ran away from for too long. My parents taught me many day-to-day skills along with a strong work ethic, but I begrudgingly acknowledged them without taking on the true meaning of the task. Being in my early twenties, I was ready to shift my mind-set to learn things I had missed out on and try to understand their meaning. I had big and small questions about life— simple, ordinary, every day wonders.

The many random questions I needed help with from God and others are the ones I hope to answer in this book. Some of the questions are simple, others are complicated, and yet others you may wonder why it's even asked. Well, some of us are blessed to receive answers quickly about life, while others tend to receive it slowly. I was the slow one, as some of these questions have only been answered in my mid-fifties as I cross over to the last half of my life.

This book has taken on a life of its own as I would say it crosses several genres: self-help, resource, personal diary.

It most likely fits all to some extent. My hope is to excite the younger ones in answering questions they have only thought of but don't want to ask, and others my age and beyond to read and nod in agreement. It also is a written history for my children and grandchildren so they know where they came from, and once they find out, they will know that only God could have changed me to be the woman I am.

In an attempt to give focus to the structure of this book, I have worked hard at sharing as if we were personally visiting. Some of my dear friends have heard these stories over coffee and I hope you can hear the passion, excitement, and encouraging zest that emanates from me as if we were sitting face to face. In my enthusiasm, I share personal stories of how God brought me to my current destination in life, along with what God has taught me with scriptures that have helped along the way.

Please join me and take this journey to explore every day simple life questions as we live in this complicated world. May God do with these words what He wants to and with whom He needs to.

Who am I?

What do you want me to be?

Where am I to work?

Complexities of Life

With all my running and gunning during my teenage years and early twenties, I was not interested in learning much from anyone because of my "I know it all attitude." I especially didn't want to learn anything from my parents, even though they taught me a lot. I was not interested in actively engaging in things that would have been of value to me at the time or in the future.

The opportunities that were presented to me to learn basic life skills and some that were extraordinary were countless. With my selfish, know-it-all attitude I pushed them all away for the life of addiction and darkness. The path that my life has taken has had many detours because of my willful thinking that I know best. By the time I escaped the negative lifestyle, my physical age was twenty-five yet my emotional age was twelve based on the time the first detour took place. Even though I surrendered by going to alcohol and drug treatment, it was only a small drop in a huge pail of an empty soul that needed to be filled. The first five years of recovery were a battle to let go of the idea that I was in control. The twelve-step program saved my life and gave me direction down a path I had no idea about, but I knew it was better than what I had experienced.

My life looked like the prisoners of old who were bound with a ball and chain to make sure they would not be able to run free. The chain represented shame, guilt, remorse, fears, anger, and resentments. The ball was the added weight of generational baggage, or what I call curses, to assure I would stay put in the wreckage of the past. As a prisoner gets shackled with the ball and chain for the first time, the intensity of the foreign object, the weight, and the obstacle it is, is noticed with every move. However, after time, movement and functionality with the ball and chain becomes easier and noticed less as the heaviness becomes normal. This is how my life felt with the weight of too many heavy chains that could never be loosened. Yet I wanted to be set free and experience what a simple life could be like with no added heaviness. Little by little each link in the chain of my bondages has been broken and freedom has been my reward.

Some of you were prisoners suffering in deepest darkness and bound by chains, because you had rebelled against God Most High and refused his advice. You were worn out from working like slaves, and no one came to help. You were in serious trouble, but you prayed to the Lord, and he rescued you.

PSALM 107:10-13 CEV

The complexity of life is insurmountable and too hard to explain all the many WHYs in life. Many, if not all, will not matter when we come to the end of our lives but the questions always remain. My life could have gone many different directions if I had not taken the detours, if I would have listened to my parents and other adults not to go down a dark path, and if I would have grabbed onto opportunities like learning how to fly an airplane, my journey of life would have been different. So after the first five years of stubborn resistance to believing in a god or Higher Power as it is referred to in the twelve-step program, I took hold of a statement that fit my black or white personality. That statement says, "God either is or He isn't, what will be your choice?" It implies that I was in control and I had a choice, so I jumped all in and said to the air and the sky, "If there is a God and you are out there, help me and show me how real you can be." The response was like someone whispering to me or me talking to myself saying, "It will be okay." The simple statement and moment was the turning point in my life of surrendering to a God I did not understand, yet who was seemingly real because I felt a sense of peace come over me like I had never experienced before.

Was my life after this experience a beautiful bed of roses neatly fenced? Absolutely NOT! As of this writing I am in my thirtieth year of recovery, and some days it feels like I am wise and the past is a million years ago. But then there are days when the enemy trips me up and I tumble into the past where I am stupid, useless, and uneducated, and it feels like only today is as much as I can handle.

The question of why I am doing this book still haunts me because of the lies the enemy tells me about who I was in my past, but the peace and the freedoms I have experienced and felt in my walk on this journey of life tell me that God's hand has been guiding me all along and I must not let go. So as my experience has shown me, hold on for dear life and go with the flow. That has been easier said than done, as I want explanations along the way. I've never experienced flashing neon lights from God with arrows or words of responses to prayers, so all I know is I keep walking and putting one foot in front of the other, trusting with all my heart that He will open the next door and shut the others.

> *I know your deeds. See, I have placed before you an open door that no one can shut. I know that you have little strength, yet you have kept my word and have not denied my name.*
>
> REVELATION 3:8 NIV

The initial WHY was to answer the question readers of my memoir *Carried by Faith* consistently asked: "How did you live life after the motorcycle accident?" Up to approximately twenty years into recovery I'd say, "Not so well." Even though I let God in my life, I was still trying to run the show by specific prayers telling God exactly what I wanted and needed by struggling personally with my belief in myself to have confidence, to be content, and to have a sense of peace. In addition, the desire in my heart was to learn God's Word, to soak up and educate myself in as much knowledge as I could glean from the Bible. Even though many of these things have happened and I have grown by leaps and bounds from where I was when I first stepped on the path of life with God, it has had many interesting rest stops placed there by God.

Fully letting go will be explained to me by God when I get to heaven; until then I will need to continue to practice it every single day. My expectations are many and my imaginative mind sets out to create some wild ideas and dreams. But I have come to realize in the last ten years the true meaning of, "I am nothing without you God." I know nothing. It's not that I'm uneducated, it's that I am beginning to understand the vastness of the God of the Universe. I don't understand the ways of the world, but I understand God's world is upside down and inside out to our earthly world. My understanding of complexity is nothing to the issues that God takes care of every millisecond of the day. And my life will be okay when I let go and live every day with simple hope in arriving in God's Kingdom when He determines my days are finished here on earth. I know there is no magic wand to make the many dreams I have come true. And I know only God will keep leading and guiding me to where and who He wants me to influence. So, I fully abandon myself to God and give Him all the power to run the remaining days of my life, if only for today.

I can do all this through him who gives me strength.
PHILIPPIANS 4:13 NIV

For God so loved the world that he gave his one and only Son, that whoever believes in him shall not perish but have eternal life.
JOHN 3:16 NIV

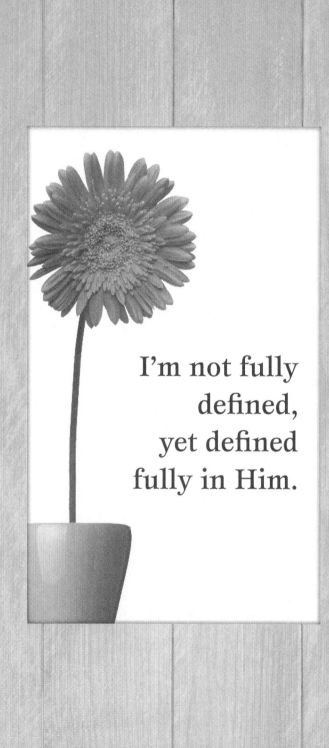

I'm not fully
defined,
yet defined
fully in Him.

Who I Am

As a little girl when I was asked, "What do you want to be when you grow up?"

My answer for many years was, "A cheerleader."

As we become older and graduate, the question changes to, "What do you do?"

This question traditionally evokes answers of a job title and place of business where we work. For most of our working careers this is a commonly asked question when we meet others. It's an easy question to ask when we don't know what to say. It's a good starting point to find out more about the person.

In American culture there is a high importance put on what a person does for their profession and the company they work for. The significance of the job position can begin to alter our thinking from what we do to earn a living to an identity of who we are. The value can start to embed in our minds and reposition what was previously a job to earn money to pay our bills to a form of being the most important thing in our lives. It can overtake us.

This transformation from "what I do" to "who I am" is where I got lost within a job title as it became my everything, my identity. The position within a company meant who I was. I was the: manager, salesperson, motivational speaker, author. My "who I am" was always tied to a job title.

As my walk with God deepened, my priorities began to reposition to see how my worth and value in God's eyes was much different than mine. As the blinders of the world loosened, my view was becoming clearer as I wanted to focus on being a wife, mom, daughter, and friend. During this time, God was making drastic changes in my world. He pulled me out and away from my identifying corporate job. To ease the transition and to work things out of me at a more comfortable pace, I started a small cleaning business. Now I was an entrepreneur, a house cleaner according to my identity with a job title in the worldly standards. I also was doing motivational speaking and writing a book, but, in my mind, I was a house cleaner. There was nothing wrong with what I was doing, but I realized how much importance I gave to it.

During this time a gnawing question came to me daily: "Who Am I?" Am I a wife, mother, house cleaner, motivational speaker, author, friend? The question increased with intensity and became more frustrating as it never left my head. On a day of total frustration, I reached out to a mentor who graciously listened and then suggested that I sit quietly and journal my question on paper to see if any answers would come to me. Sitting with my journal and pen I wrote out the words "Who Am I?" on the top of the page. The question appeared larger than life. I did not know who I was. I could only identify with the many job titles and by the skills I was able to do in each one. As the question raced in my mind, the answer was dependent on who I was around and what I thought would impress them and possibly help me get some additional business out of our conversation. I was like a chameleon, blending in with the environment adjusting to protect myself, my reputation, and my identity. Ultimately, I was becoming exhausted with these attempts to figure out what would be the best answer for the specific situation. Throwing my hands up in surrender, I knew I needed God to answer my question, "Who Am I?"

God has never taken my pen and written the words for me; I have had to go through the process. Getting to the answer was going to take action, so I began to write and these descriptive words flowed out of me: creative, positive-minded, sensitive, hard-working, authentic, spunky, caring, loving, a leader, action-minded, dependable, trustworthy, a go-getter, and honest. It was a great list of adjectives. But it didn't take away the sting of the lurking question, and I walked away from the journal frustrated.

Eight years later, as God would have it, I picked up that journal and there was the page with the big question "Who Am I?" printed in large, bold letters. Below it were the many expressive words. Why was I back to the same place in my life asking the same question which seemed bigger than life as each letter jumped off the page—WHO AM I?

During those eight years many changes happened in my life including my personal relationship with God and how important it had become. My love for His Word, the quiet time I spend daily with Him, and the studying of His truths have penetrated my heart and changed my thinking.

Now, as I sat staring at the question "Who Am I?" it seemed to have changed. By eliminating the question mark and flip flopping two words, it says, "Who I Am." The entire context changed the long-standing question. It was life changing as it jumped off the page to say "Who I am" versus "Who am I." It is now a statement, not an unanswered question. It's a statement of faith grounded in God alone. The heaviness of a wondering question has changed to a freeing statement of "This is who I am."

"Who I am" is who God says I am.

I am alive in Christ

But because of his great love for us, God, who is rich in mercy, made us alive with Christ even when we were dead in transgressions—it is by grace you have been saved.

EPHESIANS 2:4-5 NIV

I am forgiven and redeemed

In Him we have redemption through His blood, the forgiveness of sins, according to the riches of His grace.

EPHESIANS 1:7 NKJV

I am free from the law of sin and death

Therefore, there is now no condemnation for those who are in Christ Jesus, because through Christ Jesus the law of the Spirit who gives life has set you free from the law of sin and death.

ROMANS 8:1-2 NIV

I am renewed in the knowledge of God and no longer want to live my old ways

Do not lie to each other, since you have taken off your old self with its practices and have put on the new self, which is being renewed in knowledge in the image of its Creator.

COLOSSIANS 3:10 NIV

I am chosen

But you are a chosen people, a royal priesthood, a holy nation, God's special possession, that you may declare the praises of him who called you out of darkness into his wonderful light.

1 PETER 2:9 NIV

I am a new creation

Therefore, if anyone is in Christ, he is a new creation; old things have passed away; behold, all things have become new.

2 CORINTHIANS 5:17 NKJV

I am the righteousness of God

For He made Him who knew no sin to be sin for us, that we might become the righteousness of God in Him.

2 CORINTHIANS 5:21 NKJV

I am chosen

Therefore, as God's chosen people, holy and dearly loved, clothe yourselves with compassion, kindness, humility, gentleness and patience.

COLOSSIANS 3:12 NIV

I am loved

For God so loved the world that He gave His only begotten Son, that whoever believes in Him should not perish but have everlasting life.

JOHN 3:16 NKJV

I am healed

"He himself bore our sins" in his body on the cross, so that we might die to sins and live for righteousness; "by his wounds you have been healed."

1 PETER 2:24 NIV

I am called to live a holy life

He has saved us and called us to a holy life—not because of anything we have done but because of his own purpose and grace. This grace was given us in Christ Jesus before the beginning of time.

2 TIMOTHY 1:9 NIV

I am a daughter of the living God

And, "I will be a Father to you, and you will be my sons and daughters, says the Lord Almighty."

2 CORINTHIANS 6:18 NIV

These are scriptures that strengthen and remind me who God says I am. They answer the question to say, "I am whole. I am all of what God says I am when I keep my faith in God and stay close to Him."

You and I were made exactly how God intended us to be. Yet many of us vigorously fight to be what we think we should be, not what God wanted US to be. God only wants us to BE who He intended us to be. We are all ordinary, some of us will do extraordinary things in life, yet most of us will do life in a simple, nothing-special way in terms of the world's standards. But there is nothing wrong with that. In God's standard we are special, uniquely the way He made us. The uniqueness we've been given is GOD'S UNIQUENESS.

Staying faithful and being satisfied with what God has made me today, not tomorrow or yesterday. By being fully loved by God, nothing more, nothing less. *I'm not fully defined, yet defined fully in Him.* God is in me, so I am complete. He is the Vine, I am the branch. He will sustain me, direct me, lead and guide me in the journey of life. As a result of staying connected to Him, the question mark is eliminated and the uneasy feelings are gone because… "I Am Who God Says I Am."

This brings us full circle to the question asked at the beginning: "What do you do?" I am a daughter of the Most High, Loving God, who has made me uniquely ME.

In worldly definitions I will say, "I'm a cheerleader." Not the traditional one as a performer on the sidelines cheering on a sports team; no, I'm a motivational speaker and author who encourages others to make changes in their own lives to be able to boldly say, ***"I'm okay being ME, the ME, God intended ME to BE!"***

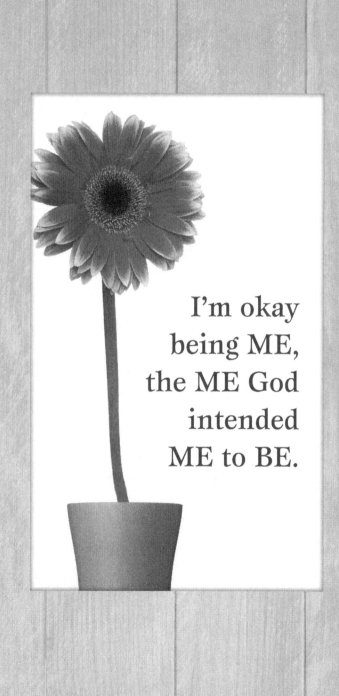

I'm okay
being ME,
the ME God
intended
ME to BE.

Uniquely Me

My yearning and search to have more in life has been relent-less and never satisfied. Wanting more is not a bad thing as it makes a person strive to better themselves. Once I made the decision to throw in the towel and gave up the orneriness of not believing there was a God, I jumped in with both feet to learn as much as a I could. It's taken many years in my walk with God to realize I will be working on my flaws up until the day I die when God welcomes me to heaven. Never being satisfied can be viewed negatively, yet I choose to look at it positively. This drive has allowed me to look at myself, my relationship with God and with others.

As the self-examining continues, I say, "I am uniquely different." Let me explain. I am unique. You are unique. We are all unique. Embracing this fact allows for freedom in who God wants us to be. Even when it's not clear on who it is.

Here's an interesting example of how to look at each per-son's uniqueness. Some people think we are to look like a set of fine china with a perfect printed pattern and all the matching pieces to show the flawless distinction that no oth-ers can have. But most of us are like dishes at a second-hand store sitting on a shelf alone with our faded pattern from years of use. The many defects are easily shown: chips, nicks, and wear marks reveal the years of living life. Yet, they sit on the shelf by themselves with a confidence and strong determination, not worrying about life because they have the strong, individual perseverance to know they will be taken care of and have a new home soon. These dishes are the unique ones, ones that are sought out for their bold, individual look, and character to stand on their own.

Embracing our uniqueness can be difficult. It's hard to accept those chips that have made us who we are. The years of wear and tear are permanent and do not go away. A few of them can be camouflaged but most of the time they cannot be covered up. Being human, we tend to strive and desire to be the perfect piece of fine china sitting beautifully on the table of life. Wanting so badly to look perfect. The flaws we see show we are not perfect, and accepting who God wants us to be is the key to understanding the different and unique way He made us.

It takes action to begin to accept ourselves. The definition of acceptance clearly states that it is the act of accepting someone or something requiring action. We need to keep on believing or at least trying to believe we are uniquely made, and when we take action it becomes easier to accept ourselves. A phrase I repeat to myself and encourage others to say BOLDLY is, "I'm okay being ME, the ME God intended ME to BE."

Looking for the ultimate acceptance by others has been a problem area my entire life. I've looked for others, "them," to validate my existence, to approve of my physical appearance, the job I held, the person I married, and the choices of my friends. The mental energy needed for this trying to please "them" when I don't even know who "them" is can be all-consuming and exhausting. But, when I focus on how uniquely I am made in God's eyes, then I don't need to care what "they" think.

This all-consuming effort in my mind has led to several unhealthy relationships in the quest to make sure that "they" approve of me. It has led me to friendships and time invested in making sure I am the best friend I can be to others. The energy given to others to make sure I am available has been tiring, making me wonder why I need to have so many friends? Why can't I be okay being by myself? Which led to another intriguing question: "How good of a friend am I to myself?" I knew the answer: "Not so good most of the time."

By examining the idea of being my own best friend, I had to ask myself, "What do I want out of these relationships? What am I looking for in others that I can't find within myself?" This was an interesting way to think about my issues—simply put, my problems. I was looking for others to daily fill me up, direct me, make me feel good about myself. This is a definition for failure and leans on the crazy side of thinking.

Growing up I always wanted to have a best friend, the B.F.F. (Best Friend Forever), a friendship where we were inseparable, in which we told our innermost secrets, the one who was my friend from grade school on, and who would be my maid of honor at my wedding. Those were little girl dreams that continued as I became a grown woman, and I would keep searching for this in every relationship I would have with other women.

During this examination of what I was looking for in others to make me satisfied, God began to press on my heart the need to ask myself a serious question, "Why don't you become your own best friend?" That was an extremely interesting question. Now, the table was turned and I was careful to review the characteristics I wanted in a best friend. Huh, kind of two-faced in a way. When evaluating myself as being my own best friend as I compared it to someone else being my best friend, the variables seemed to change. I wasn't so hard on the qualifications and the must-have attributes. I began to wonder, why should they be any different?

As I pushed through the thought process to get to an answer, I came up with a list I needed in someone to be my Best Friend Forever.

Qualities Needed
for a Best Friend Forever:

- I wanted someone to spend time with me.
- I wanted a person who would listen to me.
- I wanted someone who occasionally does special things for me.
- I wanted a person who would encourage me whenever I needed it.

With the list in hand, I wondered, "Can I do these things for myself?" To my amazement, after slowly thinking through each one, I could answer with a unanimous, "YES!" Here was a WOW moment in my life. It was a moment of clarity in my soul that I could help myself by being my own best friend.

This intriguing analysis filled me with emotions because of the revelation that I could help myself instead of looking to others to fix me. Tears streamed down my face as this earth-shattering idea hit my brain. The discovery rocked my world and I wanted to shout out loud, "I can spend time with myself." It was an eye-opening moment as it registered in my brain. The deep thinker in me needed to do further examination of each qualification to be certain I could be my own best friend.

Could I listen to myself? Well, as you have experienced in how I write, you can imagine how my thought life is in my head. The answer was a resounding, "Yes." There is a little more work to do in this area by training myself to stop my thoughts and listen more closely to what I'm saying. This discipline is challenging because it is hard to stop a run-away train. Yet, with practice, most days I am able to put the brakes on long enough to slow my thinking down and if needed I can come to a complete stop.

How was I at doing special things for myself? Yikes. I'd have to say average at best, but I do them, just not very often. The activities I enjoy that make me feel good are things like getting a pedicure, taking a walk to enjoy nature, making a good meal with a yummy dessert, and eating all of it with no guilt! This area could use some improvement because I tend to think that the items that cost money may be too expensive and I'm not worth it. But this is when I get to STOP to listen to what I'm saying to myself and redirect those thoughts to be more positive by saying, "I am worth it."

What about the area of encouraging myself? Can I be my own cheerleader? This has been a hard one as the enemy works overtime by bringing up old behaviors, shameful and guilty events, and way too often the idea that my intelligence is in question. With God's help and other wise counsel, I have developed additional skills to overcome this area of weakness and turn it into a positive. Encouraging myself with God's Word immediately inspires me to focus on what God has done in my life and brings me to a state of gratefulness. Each time, it takes less and less to have the good habits of seeking God's Word come first versus falling into the pit of destruction.

They all receive a check mark of approval as taking action in learning how to be my own best friend. Thank you, God, for this accomplishment.

Anchor Your Day

"Slow down you're going too fast!" I've been told this nearly every day of my life. My mind goes with fast moving thoughts from the moment my eyes open. I learned late in life that my day must be anchored in Christ to have constantly good days.

This hope is a strong and trustworthy anchor for our souls.
It leads us through the curtain into God's inner sanctuary.

HEBREWS 6:19 NLT

The best days are when my thoughts are centered and fixed on God being the focus of my life. Looking upward to Him to trust and let go of the firm grip of control. He is the one closest to the center of my gravity allowing me to be in the world but not of it.

The world can be twirling and spinning out of control, but when I am determined to ask God to be in my day, it will be a good one. I will be able to stand firm in the middle of the revolving chaos of life and have focus and direction. God helps me stay focused in the spinning world called LIFE when I keep clear thinking in my head and lighten my firm grip of perceived control. The words from the Message version of the Bible say it well:

Dear friend, guard Clear Thinking and Common Sense with your life; don't for a minute lose sight of them. They'll keep your soul alive and well; they'll keep you fit and attractive. You'll travel safely; you'll neither tire nor trip. You'll take afternoon naps without a worry; you'll enjoy a good night's sleep. No need to panic over alarms or surprises, or predictions that doomsday's just around the corner, because GOD will be right there with you; he'll keep you safe and sound.

PROVERBS 3:21-26 MSG

God gave me an analogy to relate to the way thoughts can overtake me. It's a grade school memory. I grew up in a small farm community and attended a small public school with class sizes of five or six students per grade; we were like family. I liked school, the teachers, and the food.... I liked it all. Recess was something I loved and remember well...running as fast as you could to the playground to claim your spot on your favorite play equipment.

My favorite, the metal giant, the merry-go-round, sat patiently waiting for all the kids to climb on it. There were three positions you could claim: runner, sitter, or center. The runner would push and run at the same time, making the metal circle go as fast as possible. I'd always hope there were a few strong boys who wanted to be the runner because they would get it going so fast, you'd have to hang on for dear life. They'd make it fly and sometimes you'd feel sick after recess. The sitter would strategically place themselves in-between the metal bars with legs folded in and feet tucked under for stability. You needed to make sure you weren't too close to the outside edge of the wheel because there was a tendency to come loose and fall off. When I was the sitter, I'd be ready to enjoy the ride making sure to keep my eyes closed, not even taking a little peek because at times you'd spin so fast you'd get dizzy. The center was the prime position, the closest to the center of gravity. It was an amazing spot to be in because you could stand straight up with your hands in the air and even open your eyes and not fall. This by far was the place I wanted to be. But with only one spot available, it was the hardest to get if you weren't the fastest out of the classroom.

My life has felt like the merry-go-round as life spins so fast with all the responsibilities and different obligations: being a mom of young children, a new job, financial pressures, health issues, elderly parents, and possibly death. There are days I'm the runner—pushing and running as fast as I can. These days are exhausting and overwhelming. I find little satisfaction and question myself, "Why am I doing what I'm doing?" I can barely hang on and I feel that I may fall off. Other days, I'm the sitter—quietly sitting feeling secure with the ride of life. Being content at the quietness around me and being able to see the joys of life. I can feel the fast pace around yet I'm free in the turmoil, allowing it to simply pass by.

The way I have learned how to stay focused and not begin the spinning is to be intentional each day by doing basic and foundational activities that set my day on a good course. These are simple, core habits which have changed my life for the better, allowing me not to rush, rather stroll, through my day giving me peace while I allow God to lead and me to follow.

Anchors to Start Your Day

Set an Alarm

Choose a wake-up time that allows for room to get things done that are important and set the day off to a good start. The amount of time needed is up to each person, may it be two hours or thirty minutes. Being reminded of the goal to not rush, giving time to God so there is breathing room to be calm so the still, small voice can be heard for the plans of the day. When the BUZZ is heard, praise God for another day, thanking Him, telling Him how much He is loved.

Get Out of Bed

When the alarm goes off—GET UP! It's simple. Only hit snooze once on those days you're super tired. Hitting snooze one too many times will make the day run behind no matter how our well-intended, planned out day was to go. On the days that are a challenge to rise and shine, this "oldie but goodie" song can help get a person up and going—*Rise and shine and give God the glory, rise and shine and give God the glory, glory. Rise and shine and give God the glory, children of the Lord.*

Make Your Bed

Why? The biggest reason is so you won't get back in it! It takes mere seconds to do and it makes the room look nice and tidy, even if you don't see it again until you go to bed.

Get Moving

Exercise. This is covered in the chapter Keep Moving.

Cool Down

Turn the 10-minute cool-down from exercising into lunch prep for yourself, kids, or your spouse. Make sure they are packed with love and an encouraging note. See Appendix Lunch Love Notes for ideas.

God Time

Time spent with God can be the best part of the day. Sitting still, opening up to God, uncovering our needs, and leaning into what He may have for us to do this day even if we can only give Him five minutes. Ideas for this time are reading a devotion, journaling, Bible reading, and prayer for kids, spouse, and others.

Get Dressed

Shower and go time. Keeping it simple in your getting ready routine is a must. We can be simple and still be stylish. It's helpful to pick out what to wear the night before even if it's only in your mind. While you're getting dressed in the morning, use this practical application referring to the Armor of God to remember the verses and visualize the impact of each piece of armor and the benefit gained from it.

For more details on the Armor of God, check out Getting Dressed Prayer on page 117.

*Be strong in the Lord and in his mighty power. **Put on** all of God's armor so that you will be able to **stand firm** against all strategies of the devil. For we are not fighting against flesh-and-blood enemies, but against evil rulers and*

ities of the unseen world, against mighty powers
dark world, and against evil spirits in the heav-
enly places. Therefore, **put on** *every piece of God's armor*
so you will be able to resist the enemy in the time of evil.
Then after the battle **you will still be standing firm.**
Stand *your ground,* **putting on** *the belt of truth and the*
body armor of God's righteousness. For shoes, **put on** *the*
peace that comes from the Good News so that you will be
fully prepared. In addition to all of these, **hold up** *the*
shield of faith to stop the fiery arrows of the devil. **Put**
on *salvation as your helmet, and* **take** *the sword of the*
Spirit, which is the word of God. **Pray** *in the Spirit at*
all times and on every occasion. **Stay alert** *and be per-*
sistent in your prayers for all believers everywhere.

EPHESIANS 6:10-18NLT

The last action to take is to kiss, hug, pray, and say "I love you" to each other as we release one another into our busy, separate ways for the day. The tradition of praying for our kids and saying "I love you" can become a daily routine with a short and to the point prayer that only takes a few seconds—asking for God's hand to be upon them to keep them healthy, safe, and strong, in Jesus name, AMEN.

When these steps are done before I walk out the door each day, they help set the anchor. It takes discipline as we can wade into apathy and laziness. But when they are done consistently, the results will be a firm foundation on which a successful life is built.

God Time

Keeping close to God like I would a person in the flesh was the only way I could wrap my head around how to keep taking the next step in improving my relationship with God. Trusting Him for every move I made was what I needed to do in becoming the new woman He desired me to be. My well-worn path of the habit of trying to control was comfortably familiar because it allowed me to know where I was going. The new direction of following God's lead was scary because I felt lost in the wilderness without a compass. Keeping it simple by staying in the day, putting one foot in front of the next, and trusting God was like having a compass placed in my hands. Now learning how to follow His lead to an unknown place was difficult. It had to be kept simple with only one-step directions at a time. The only way to get the directions was to continue to know God like a friend.

Talking to Him as I would a friend had to be normal and comfortable—compared to what was easier as I sought out others to fill me, to give me reassurance, confidence, strength, and understanding so I could do the next thing in my day. I would spill my guts with honesty, telling my inner-most feelings and hurts so they could understand me and give me advice, guidance, and direction in the way I needed to go. In every encounter of this type of personal exposure, it would eventually leave me feeling like a semi-deflated helium balloon. Immediately, I would feel like a fully filled balloon, but after a few days the deflation came and I would feel weak, like I was dying. I felt like there was no life, no basis for existence, no hope for the future.

Repeatedly I would try to find just the right person to whom I could express just the right words to explain my feelings, anguishes, dreams, and hopes. But time and time again, the picture of the balloon slowly deflating was how my soul felt. The pain of bearing myself to others in hopes they would be the right person to help this tattered soul was arrogant and foolish on my part. No human can ever help elevate the hurts and pains of another. Yet in my humanness, I truly believed it was possible.

There finally came a realization as God tapped me on the shoulder and said, "Are you done yet? Are you ready to let Me fill you up?" The constant need for others to try and fix me and give me all I needed was on the verge of crazy. The constant searching and seeking out of others to fill me up vanished once this awareness hit my core thoughts. My soul was beginning to feel His pure presence. I longed to be filled with God. God was doing for me what neither I nor anyone else could do for me. He was filling me with His mighty strength, His confidence, His overflowing love. **His fullness was filling my emptiness.**

I sensed and felt the overwhelming love and commitment only our Heavenly Father can give us. Love so unspeakable, joy overflowing, passion exploding, confidence abounding, and love never ending. I had to run to the end of the course in seeking Him in everybody and everything else. I had to see the end of the rope and walk to the end of the plank so there was nothing else left. And there He was, sitting patiently waiting for me. For me to finally realize He was the way, the truth, and the life I had always been seeking. The voids were being filled. The gaps were closing in on one another by Him and Him alone.

This new idea was a process and did not happen overnight. When the urge came to call someone to blab my troubles to, I would try and capture the thought and redirect it to God. When I was able to catch myself, it was a sign of growth in refocusing, and in new Godly direction. To impose self-control on my strong human urges that wanted to kidnap me and take me back to the old behavior, I had to call on **G**od **O**rderly **D**irection. My new priority had to be going to my one TRUE friend, God.

He had to be my Best Friend Forever! The one and only true friend, the lover of my soul, my kindred spirit, the one who keeps me sane, who loves me when I can't love myself. The one who builds me up when I'm in shambles, who settles my shaken soul, who calms my crazy thoughts, and gives me unspeakable peace. The one who explains and justifies why I am the way I am. The one who knocks my socks off in accepting me the way I am with all the imperfections. The one who loves me until my soul feels so full and who penetrates my heart with love, understanding, and mercy.

To finally come to the understanding that He is the one who accepts me fully as I am makes me explode with awe. He made me who I am, with all my faults and imperfections, to use me to try to explain how madly in love He is with each of us. Caressing and touching the aching, broken places of our hearts and souls. Filling cracks and spaces of the years of feeling abandoned, lost, and betrayed, with tender, loving hope of eternity only coming from Him.

> *No longer do I call you servants, for the servant does not know what his master is doing; but I have called you friends, for all that I have heard from my Father I have made known to you.*
>
> JOHN 15:15 ESV

The amazement of what God does once we fully let Him take over is astonishing. He uses tattered, broken souls and mends them into beautiful, loving people who can help others find Him. Taking no personal credit and simply being willing to let God keep working on us is the point in life, opening the soul to the one who knows. To have His way, to mold and reform us to the person He wants us to be. To allow His work to be done in me, to know the next move, by being close enough to hear His still, small voice. This daily practice of letting Him direct and set the course on the journey is one of comfort. To know He's got my back, He won't let me down, He has plans to prosper and not harm me. The Void is Filled.

> *....and after the fire a still small voice.*
>
> 1 KINGS 19:12 NKJV

How do we develop a relationship with God as our best friend? Just like we would with a friend in the flesh; connecting with them by spending time together, listening, talking, venting, sharing frustrations, and excitement. The best thing to do is to imagine what we do with our friends here on earth; this is the way to think of how we develop our relationship with God.

God Time Developing Tips

Five Minutes to Come Alive

Give five minutes to God each day. The first small step is to set aside a time duration that works for you. During this time sit quietly to release your thoughts and clear the busyness. If five minutes feels like eternity, stop at the two-minute mark and work up to five minutes. Keep working at it and the time will increase as the rewards of giving your time to God begins to make a difference in your life.

Same Time

Choosing the same time each day to spend time with God is a key to success. Morning is the best time as it is clearly stated in scripture. There is truth to the scriptures and when it specifically instructs us to rise early in the morning to find a solitary place to communicate with God, then we need to do it.

"Very early in the morning, while it was still dark, Jesus got up, left the house and went off to a solitary place, where he prayed."

MARK 1:35 NIV

Our Space

When we feel comfortable and have all the necessary items close by, the chances for success in remaining still and allowing God to be with us will be more likely.

Comfortable Space

Create a cozy, quiet place where you feel safe.

Surround Yourself with Useful Items

Investing in these items can allow for more growth as you search yourself and the relationship with God.

Bible

Find one of your choice and invest the money into purchasing it. A personal favorite is the Life Application Bible —New International Version. There are so many versions to choose from. The key is to find the one that fits you. It's okay if you buy several different versions so you can have them all available while studying. Or you could buy a parallel bible which is good because it has three or four versions in one book.

Tabs

Adding tabs to a Bible is important if it doesn't already come with it. This is a great investment and will elevate stress as you learn the Books of the Bible.

Bible App for Phone

There are many apps for mobile phones for quick referencing as you begin to study the Bible more.

Devotional

Finding one among the many to choose from can be a challenge. One of my favorites is *Jesus Calling* by Sarah Young.

Other Spiritual Books

The list is endless of Christian authors who have insight on a variety of topics. Explore what types of books you'd enjoy and have a few available to read so you can change up your pattern of quiet time. There are times we can feel we are in a rut with our time we spend with God. This is when we need to pick up some other good Christian material to fill our minds.

Journal

This is for writing daily entries about your life, writing out prayers or scripture, and writing out verses that jump out at you during your study time.

Reference Resources

A dictionary, concordance, etc. These are help mates for working deep into God's Word.

Prayer Cards

A.k.a. recipe cards, are a must when we want to keep praying for the loved ones in our lives on an ongoing basis. Having one for each person in the family helps to remember the specific requests that are turned up to God. Once the prayer is on paper and visible, it's easier to grab and read often. Prayer is the lifeline to God. It helps keep our sanity when worry takes over. I say, "When worry comes, it must be turned to prayer."

Coffee Mug

Coffee is a must and if you're like me it needs to be a large coffee mug. Enough to enjoy the time set aside with God.

Music

Entering into God's presence is often done by listening to music which can help us feel closer to God. The options are endless so take time to listen to the style of worship music you like.

The focus of the time spent with God can vary for each person. Remember He is our friend and is ready to hear whatever we need to talk about. God is waiting with love and grace for the things we need to share. Releasing our heaviness, our situations which feel impossible, and asking for help is what He waits for, the action of placing everything before Him to finally say, "I give up."

Actions to Release
Our Circumstances

Surrender

Give all your burdens to God who knows all and will NEVER forsake us.

> *Be strong! Be courageous! Do not be afraid of them! For the Lord your God will be with you. He will neither fail you nor forsake you.*
>
> DEUTERONOMY 31:6 TLB

Rise Up

Rise above the emotional mess and move on. Only in God can strength be found.

> *Fear not, for I am with you. Do not be dismayed. I am your God. I will strengthen you; I will help you; I will uphold you with my victorious right hand.*
>
> ISAIAH 41:10 TLB

Persevere

To achieve something despite difficulties, failure, or opposition, we must press forward and never give up.

> *Happy is the man who doesn't give in and do wrong when he is tempted, for afterwards he will get as his reward the crown of life that God has promised those who love him.*
> JAMES 1:12 TLB

Working on these action steps will help us stay positive and know God is the only one who can help us. The results will be visible in our daily lives by refusing to fall into negative talk or becoming frustrated when we have a setback. By focusing on taking these steps one day at a time, and practicing them repeatedly, we will learn how to catch ourselves and pull ourselves up and out. We can survive and thrive!

Once you have committed to try these ideas and to take action you will see results. They may be quick or they could be slow, but they will happen when you are committed to giving it your all. God will meet you when you meet Him. The list of what we receive when we spend time with God is endless.

Results of Spending Time with God

- Calming a busy mind
- Quiet, peaceful mind
- The Bible will come alive and make sense
- A deep personal relationship with God will develop
- Hearing God's still, small voice

Don't take my word for it regarding what your results will be when you give God your time; read it in the Bible and hear the promises. Take the challenge and see how your relationship with God develops so you can say, "God, you are my B.F.F. (Best Friend Forever)!"

> *"I am with you and will watch over you where you go, and I will bring you back to this land. I will not leave you until I have done what I promised you."*
>
> GENESIS 28:15 NIV

> *"I will give you a new heart and put a new spirit in you; I will remove from you your heart of stone and give you a heart of flesh."*
>
> EZEKIEL 36:26 NIV

Obedient Wife

Before my husband and I were married in the church, it was required we meet with the priest for marriage counseling for a few weeks. At this time, our distinct differing views were expressed to the priest. During one of our last sessions, he gave us some scriptures he recommended for our wedding ceremony and asked us to look them over to see which ones we preferred.

When I got home and began to read them, I was enraged! Many of them had the O word in them. There was no way I would let the O word be read! I had already told my future husband the O word would not be read during our wedding. He laughed, knowing I would never be the O word type of wife and expected me to voice this clearly with the priest. The O word is OBEDIENT.

Of course, none of those scriptures with the word obedient were read at our wedding. I made sure of it, in very plain language to the priest, "This woman of the '80s is not going to be under her husband's thumb and be obedient." For heaven's sake—if these were read during our wedding, it could possibly mean I would have to do it or be it—not me!

Fast forward to around ten years of marriage…we had asked Jesus into our hearts and had begun to work at having a closer relationship with God. And guess what happened—the O word came back up. I had read it in the Bible, but would quickly jump over the words and turn the page and say to myself, "No way will this ever be me."

My attitude toward being obedient to my husband was even worse than it was at the beginning of our marriage. My flesh and secular viewpoints over the years had strengthened my belief in the freedoms and rights I had as a woman born in a culture of 'I am woman, hear me roar.' I had NO intention of accepting the O word. Little did I know God was just beginning to do a work in me about the issue.

My stubbornness and ornery attitude had helped me persevere in many life situations. I believed they made me successful and gave me a "never give up" attitude and willingness to keep on pushing ahead. And YET they were crippling me at times. But I had several wonderful, patient women of God come alongside me and pass on their biblical wisdom. They were gentle at trying to convince me to view things differently and to limit my questioning of WHY I should. There's nothing wrong with questioning when you're willing to change, but if not, it can be detrimental. Going to the Word of God to receive answers gives it to me straight, and this is how I pushed through the obedient issue. It says it well in the gospel of John:

Those who accept my commandments and obey them are the ones who love me. And because they love me, my Father will love them. And I will love them and reveal myself to each of them.

JOHN 14:21 NLT

I was beginning to understand God's good, orderly direction in His kingdom and the need for obedience toward Him and others. I began to pray for obedience with God and my husband. My concept of being an obedient wife was skewed, so God began to help me find ways to understand it so it would become etched in my heart and mind. He dealt with me gently and consistently as He began to change old thought and behavior patterns through an impressionable assignment.

God laid on my heart to pack a lunch for my husband every day. This was extremely challenging as it meant I needed to get up earlier, sacrifice some of *my time*, and not complain verbally or with my body language. It was one of the biggest challenges I had endured up to that time in our marriage.

If I was going to embark on this project, I decided the details would be on my terms and I would make him lunch whenever it was convenient for me with the minimum of doing it twice a week. In God's world I've found I have absolutely NO control of what my infamous mind creates as the guidelines for a request from God. A twice a week attempt turned into every day along with the burden of an already busy schedule that did not work into *my* life.

And so the assignment started. It felt like years, but it was probably only a few weeks and I hated this entire idea. What was God doing in me? Why did I have to do it this way? What good would come of this task? Only anger? Until one day to my surprise, while my husband was on the phone, I overheard him say, "It's great to have my wife take time every day to make me lunch. And she writes me a special hand-written note that is different every day." I had to let those words settle in my mind and heart. Wow! Was this the effect this act of obedience was having on him? My husband's words of delight left a positive effect on me and began to melt my hard heart. Until I heard the conversation, I did not realize how important and what an impact the lunch and note were to him. This act of kindness, an expression of love and gratitude for him, was filling up his love tank each day.

This was a stripping of my ego, pride, and self-centeredness and has made me a more obedient individual and wife. Yes, I said it; it's in black and white—an OBEDIENT WIFE! When my prayer to God was made to help me become more obedient, I wanted to have my heart changed but I didn't know to what extent I would be transformed. God remolded me into a different woman by asking me to make lunches and write love notes.

It has been many years since this O assignment was given and one I continue to do each day for my husband. It ranks up at the top as a life-changing event for my husband and myself. It has changed me forever, and these are the benefits I have received:

Benefits of Obedience

- Found a true freedom
- Opened doors to God's care
- Led to God's glory
- Can lead to other miracles

- Led to peace
- Helped combat temptation

Timing, attitude, and prayer are essential elements to possess before embarking on an assignment like this one. I would love to tell each of you to start doing this very same assignment and you will get the same exact results. But that would be foolish. As it is with God, He directs our own individual paths to the exact direction He wants us to go. This story may trigger your own ideas to begin working on the obedience issue or the need for kindness and servanthood. For others, this exact example is one that will fit and work well for your spouse.

This O assignment has not been easy or one I've wanted to jump up and down about every single morning. There are times when I had a bad attitude and felt like putting something not so nice in his lunch. A little spite I can't seem to get 100 % rid of, but God has continued to work on me. Oh well, its progress, not perfection!! When I catch myself having a sour attitude, I remind myself how I would love it if someone made me lunch and how enjoyable it must be to open it up and find new things or a special note each day.

Lunchbox Love Notes

- Thank you for the great man of God you have become. God has changed you so much.
- Thank you for being a great, encouraging father.
- Thank you for being a loving, caring husband.

- Thanks for being an awesome man of God and great provider.

- Thank you for making our home such a beautiful place to live! God has given you many talents and for that I am very grateful!

- May God shine down on you today and make your day prosperous.

- You are the light in my day—I love to see you and hug you.

- You are a very hard worker. We so appreciate all you do for us. Thank you for being a great provider for our family.

- Thank you for being my friend and loving husband who takes such good care of me.

- Thanks for being a great man of God. Keep doing what God's telling you.

- Let's keep praying for clear direction for our future and where God wants us to be. If peace is present, we will know it's right.

- Love the day the Lord has given—cherish small moments and see them as God sees them.

- Let God be your sunshine today.

- Thanks for treating me like a queen. I know you love me, and I thank God for your love.

- Live for today. Find all the joys in this wonderful life God gave us.

- Thank you for being home every night so I don't worry or wonder where you are.
- You are my one and only shining knight.
- May love and peace be part of your day.
- Another day to rejoice in what God has given us! Thank you for being a great man of God.
- Allow God to lead you today and take His hand.
- I pray for peace and contentment for you today.
- You bless me every day by how much you show love to me and the boys. We are sooo blessed.

Offense is a fancy way to say "I'M ANGRY."

Nine

Offended Wife

Early in our marriage, we visited a counselor and after many sessions she told us, "I don't want to see the two of you anymore." We couldn't believe she said such a statement. But given that she had listened to the bantering back and forth like a ping pong ball with the typical "He said, She said" type of bickering tangent, any mature adult would tire of the battle. Each week we were given assignments to work on and report back to her on how it went, yet we would come to the session and destroy each other in her presence. She had had enough, as little progress was being made. She added to her statement a powerful realization that has never been forgotten, "Someone needs to give in and stop the arguing. There will not always be a winner and a loser." Neither of us wanted to lose.

We never went back to any marriage counselors through our years together. We have trudged through rough times of not speaking to each other for days and waiting to see who was going to *win* and who would *lose*. In the battle, neither of us wants to give in and call a truce. We have stumbled and fumbled through trials and errors of what works for us and what doesn't.

When you've been in marriage for several years, you know well what the other likes and dislikes. We are in tune to what can set the other person off to become irritated, frustrated, or angry. But one of the hardest issues to overcome is offense and working at not being OFFENDED.

Offense is a nice word for anger, resentment, or bitterness. It can be dressed up with different words yet it comes down to the same thing...OFFENSE. The definition is a feeling of anger and a failure to show regard for others. Well, I can simplify it by saying, "Offense is a fancy way to say I'm ANGRY."

Easily becoming angry has been a core feeling I've dealt with for many years. I've had many troubling tantrums with God, asking why this and why that and simply just having a fit because I'm not getting my way. He's tested and tested me again to see how I react in a situation with my husband and others. What I have discovered is when my feelings get hurt, I want to retaliate with anger, becoming offended and spitting out words that will hurt just like I feel the pain. This tends to happen when I feel put down because of my lack of knowledge on a subject, when I am caught off guard, or when I am tired. If one of these happens, my strong will kicks in to defend myself for a battle to win or lose.

God has taught me that I do not have to be offended; I have a choice. Through the testing I have fumbled and fallen, said words I wish I hadn't, and apologized more than I'd like to. What I've learned is a statement I say when I feel anger rising: "I have a choice to be offended or not."

I have had plenty of practice in making the decision to not be offended and here is what I try to do:

Steps to Stop Offense

Pause

Stop, think about what happened. This takes the form of walking away, going to the bathroom, saying a prayer, shaking off what just happened, and suiting up with God's Armor to win the battle of Not Being Offended.

Use the "I" Statement vs. "You" Statement

"I feel I'm not heard." "My feelings get hurt when we don't try to understand each other's perspective." "I'm having a hard time understanding." "I need this explained again so I can try to understand."

This is one of the most challenging things to try to do. It's more natural to examine the other person's flaws and tell them everything they are doing wrong instead of looking inward at how it makes me feel.

Clean My Side of the Street

Take my own inventory of character defects before I judge yours. I cannot keep sweeping my flaws under the rug because they will be a big lump. I try to take the magnifying glass I've examined you with and turn it back on myself. I usually find a flaw or two and ultimately say to myself, "What is my part in this disagreement?"

See if there is any offensive way in me, and lead me in the way everlasting.

PSALM 139:24 NIV

Have Gratitude

Finding or reminding myself of the positive things in the person or situation versus the negativity. This helps take the sting out of the hurting arrows that are penetrating my heart. This is when this step becomes very difficult to do while you're in the heat of the moment. This is when you must go back to Step One: PAUSE.

Break the Silence

In a battle that is building, say something to break the silence. The statement can be anything, on any subject matter, just as long as the silence is broken. With lots of practice I have found that using a statement that has nothing to do with what is being talked about is effective. Silence is the ingredient for continued separation and division, one the enemy wants to keep going. Once the silence has stopped, talking can begin again.

Unity

Keeping togetherness in a relationship is the key to staying united. No matter the differences, realizing there can be an end to division can hopefully outweigh personal stubbornness. Asking myself if it's worth the friction to keep distance and division between myself and the person or situation is the key to keep offense and anger away.

These steps really do work. God has allowed me to recognize when to use them and that they can be extremely effective. Here is an example of how a particular situation allowed me to make a decision whether I would be offended or I would be a new kind of winner.

On a beautiful sunny spring day, I was outside ready to water the garden. We have a large yard and I needed to connect many water hoses together to reach our two garden areas. A few days prior, I had noticed one of the connections leaked quite extensively so I laid this portion of the hose inside the raspberry patch to let them get a nice drink of water while I watered the rest of the garden. During this time of watering, my husband noticed me placing this water hose in the raspberries and asked me, "What are you doing?" I responded, "The connection is leaking, and I thought instead of watering the weeds, I'd give the raspberries some water." I was proud of myself because he had gotten frustrated with me at watering the weeds before with the leaking hoses. I knew he'd be happy with my decision today. NOT! His response: "Why would you do that? Why not fix the bad connection? Plus, you didn't put the hose away the right way the other day." My reaction was immediate and spoken out loud, "What? I thought you'd be glad I was watering the raspberries instead of the weeds. And the reason I didn't put the hose away was because I forgot." Wham Bam! Yep, immediately the gas got poured on my simmering embers of anger.

The argument was ready to get to the hot flame stage. What was my choice going to be? I chose to look down, hide my tears pouring from my eyes, and walk away. I sauntered slowly to the other garden to get away from him and try to stop the tears and decide how I would continue. As I walked around the garden trying to refocus and calm my crazy mind, I noticed new growth beginning in the garden, the potatoes were sprouting. By this time, he had come out to where I was. It was my opportunity, I knew I could do it, I could be the WINNER. Out of my mouth came, "Did you see we have potatoes sprouting up?" I broke the silence; I said the first words to stop the battle, the argument, and the enemy from continuing the separation game. I'm the WINNER because I've taken God's wisdom to heart and quit playing the game by choosing gentle words instead of harsh, mean-spirited ones.

> A *gentle answer deflects anger, but harsh words make tempers flare.*
>
> PROVERBS 15:1 NLT

As the wise words of Proverbs written mostly by Solomon say so gracefully, gentle words versus harsh ones will deflect anger. Proverbs uses provoking analogies to help me refocus my critical, argumentative thinking and to rethink my word choices, behaviors, and actions.

The change in how I choose to respond has happened slowly, but it's happened. It has taken practice, staying connected to God, reading the Word, and being willing to let God work on my character defects. I can see progress over the years, from a young, wild, rebellious woman who always wanted to be the WINNER, to the wise, now gray-haired woman who is willing to deflect with gentle words to gain the freedom of not being offended.

Marriage Teeter Totter

We set our eyes on each other when I was sixteen and he was twenty-one; it was love at first sight. Haha! That would be a great first sentence in a fairytale fiction book about young love but not in this book.

We met through a mutual friend and we really didn't care for each other. He had a sarcastic personality and would jab at comments I made. He was a big city guy and I was a small-town girl who grew up on a farm. We had very little in common, except the mutual friend who introduced us. He was interested in our mutual friend, so I was just the tag-along, younger friend. The rest of the story details can be read in *Carried by Faith*. We have been together since 1982 and have been through many ups and downs, a cliche, so it would be better stated that we've been on a teeter totter.

Those of you who remember the old wooden teeter totters that every elementary school had in the 1970s will have the correct picture in your head for this analogy. Those of you who are younger will need to look it up online to find a picture to help you envision the object.

In elementary school everyone would run outside to reach their favorite playground equipment to play on during recess. Mine was the merry-go-round and the teeter totter both which needed to have at least two people involved to make it fun. The teeter totters were constructed of a heavy piece of wood about twelve feet long and two inches thick, at each end there were curves on each side in which to place your legs, and on top was a metal bar to hold on. The idea was to find a partner who was close to you in size so it would be balanced evenly in weight to make the up and down motion a nice ride. It was often challenging to find the right partner to make it balance well, and many times you'd have to deal with whoever reached the teeter totter at the same time you did. On a good day, all was fine because your usual partner and you arrived at the same time and the ride was enjoyable for the entire recess. On other days, you'd get a partner that was bigger and not like you and it was a rough ride. They would try to bounce you off by leveraging their weight and strength to make their end hit the ground as hard as they could tolerate with hopes to knock you off and send you flying to the ground. If you got an equally ornery play-mate and this action started taking place, you'd be going up and down and slamming the ground repeatedly while both of you hung on as tightly as you could with neither getting knocked off. It was a rough ride because you had to hang on so tight and fight with all the muscles you had to stay on as you both went up and down.

This is how our marriage has been. One of us on the tee-ter totter hitting on the ground and the other nearly being knocked off and wanting to give up, yet both holding on as tight as we could and not being willing to give up to be thumped to the ground. The hard hits to the ground have included both of us going through addiction treatment, the birth of a son who arrived too early and who nearly died two times within a few months of his birth, financial challenges because of risks we took (some were imposed by God to help us become wiser), and many more examples which have tested our marriage.

As we close in on being together forty years, we are more like the enjoyable ride on the teeter totter when the right partner is on the other end. We are evenly balanced, we know how the other one moves and takes action, we can sense a slight shift when they need to reposition, and we know when we are tired and need to rest and be done for a period of time. You can say we are a well-run, old couple who knows what works and what doesn't.

It takes time to get to this stage of marriage; it doesn't happen within the first few years. I thought I knew my husband well after being with him the first ten years, then we started to have several bumps. Our individual personalities started shining through as the comfortable stage of marriage sank in. Life challenges hit us, like in any marriage, and blaming the other person seemed so much easier. This was the time when it would have been easy to simply walk away. We stuck it out.

In the last five years I've humorously said, "Now there is no turning back; you're stuck with me and I'm stuck with you. If you don't like it, too bad." These difficult times have allowed us to get to know each other better, and through sticking it out, we love each other more. An example of sticking it out while we don't necessarily agree is the task of working on a project together. We both have shining, bright, strong personalities who know exactly what needs to be done and we both have great leadership qualities, but that tends to lead to a difficult time together because we both think we are right and don't want to listen to the other person's ideas. In all the years we've been together, there has been no magical wand waved over us to make the situation any better during a difficult time. The thing that has changed is that we've gotten tired of the fighting against each other during these work projects and have decided to approach them differently.

Here's how the truth was spoken by my husband recently before we started a project that was going to take several days. In a loving, caring voice he said, "Okay, you know we are going to argue, but let's not start right away!" Inside I laughed, yet I knew the truth was being spoken. We know each other well and need to remind each other of our weak tendencies so we don't distance ourselves to the opposite side of the room. As the project progressed, on the first day it went well with many times of give and take. There was laughter when there could have been scrawls and many encouraging words when mistakes took place. But, as fatigue set in and safeguards lowered, offense snuck in and old behaviors came out. Like the teeter totter ride of youth when one of us got tired and made a hard bump on the ground as it nearly knocked the other person off, it was time to slow down, realign ourselves, and continue with the ride until the bell rang.

In marriage our life is back and forth, give and take through the entire marriage, NOT just the beginning years. It must be all the way to the end when God takes us home to be with Him in heaven. As men and women will view things differently through many situations in our lives, we will always be similar enough to relate and understand each other, yet different enough to butt heads. It's when one of the people chooses NOT to give and take and simply wants to knock the other person off the teeter totter and be done to find another partner is when it gets really rough.

One of the hardest parts of marriage life is when one partner doesn't want to play anymore and decides to walk away. When marriage is entered into, it doesn't mean that we ride on coast mode, let everything go, think no additional work is needed, and it will all work out by itself. No, marriage takes on a life of its own. There has to be give and take, understanding and love, along with good and tough times. God wants us to be together, to work with each other, and to be helpers for one another. He made us to be together from the beginning of time.

The Lord God said, "It is not good for the man to be alone. I will make a helper suitable for him."

GENESIS 2:18 NIV

So the Lord God caused the man to fall into a deep sleep; and while he was sleeping, he took one of the man's ribs and closed up the place with flesh. Then the Lord God made a woman from the rib he had taken out of the man, and he brought her to the man. The man said, "This is now bone of my bones and flesh of my flesh; she shall be called 'woman,' for she was taken out of man." For this reason a man will leave his father and mother and be united to his wife, and they will become one flesh.

GENESIS 2:21-24 NIV

As we've grown in our marriage so has our friendship. We've come to know ourselves and each other better through the times of give and take. Realizing we can do all things together when God is in it. It's three strands working together that makes us strong; God, my husband and me. Our relationship is not one from a fairy tale, but I'm believing it will end with the traditional, "They lived happily ever after."

Tips for a Successful Married Life

- Get up early to spend time with God.
- Exercise to look and feel good.
- Get dressed to look your best.
- Make him lunch and write a special encouraging love note.
- Kiss him goodbye and tell him you love him.
- Pick up the house, less stress.
- Plan your meals, less stress.
- Welcome and greet him as he gets home.
- Eat and pray together at meals.
- Do dishes together to spend time together talking.

- Always hug and kiss him before going to sleep.
- Tell him how much he means to you.

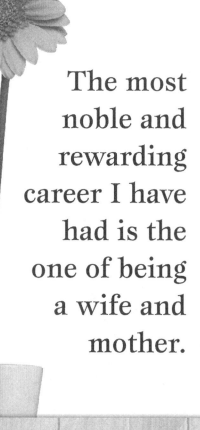

The most noble and rewarding career I have had is the one of being a wife and mother.

Making Me the Woman God Intended Me to Be

A question every child is asked is, "What do you want to be when you grow up?" My response varied through my elementary years: cheerleader, cook, hotel and restaurant manager. I never was interested in two particular occupations that some of my friends would often give as an answer: an elementary school teacher or a wife and mom. I didn't believe being a wife and mother was a career. My view of a successful job was one that looked good in the world's eye, then it would qualify me to say, "*I am somebody.*"

I was born in the 1960s, grew up in the 1970s, and hit college in the 1980s where the famous statement rang loud in strong-willed, young women's ears: "I am woman, hear me roar." It was blaring and clear to young women to stand up for your equal rights, make yourself known, climb the corporate ladder with the men to get the same pay, and before you bear children think twice about what it could do to your status in the workplace. This concept was easy for me to grasp as I was a tomboy and a hard worker and wanted nothing more than to prove myself in a man's world. Striving to be this type of woman was easy because of the background I came from. I was a fighter and had a huge amount of pride to show others I could be somebody in the world.

When it came to the idea of becoming a mother and raising children, the nurturing and mothering gene in me was weak. I had little interest in having children; they were low on my priority list. My focus was college, career, marriage, and maybe children after I accomplished these goals. My attitude toward my husband who wanted children was, "I'll let you know when I'm ready." I was cold and unemotional to my husband's desires and I would toy with his feelings by saying, "I'll think about having a baby," knowing full well I had no intention. When his pressure became stronger, I would make sure he knew who was in control of my body and say, "I'm the one who controls my body. I'm never having any children. End of story. No more discussion." My responses were short and to the point—there would be no children.

The reason why I did not want to bring children into this world was because of my selfish focus on ME and what I wanted out of life. It was all about being successful in a career, to have plenty of money in the bank, and to buy possessions to outwardly look better than others. These were my goals and I was motivated to make sure they happened, so I thought everyone should get out of my way because I would be accomplishing them all before the age of forty. Getting sidetracked from my goals would not happen. However, in a weak moment, I gave in to my husband's continual nagging about the need to start a family.

My compromise was the willingness to have only one child because I believed I could handle one based on my ability to successfully manage a multi-million-dollar department and oversee many employees within a successful company.

One child later, a whole new world opened up in me: motherhood. My self-centered desires I yearned for in the corporate world were turned upside down and inside out once I gazed into the eyes of our firstborn son. I fell head over heels in love with this tiny human and saw life from a different perspective. This beautiful child who was formed in my womb from a small cell of two separate individuals was now making me analyze my entire life focus. He would soon call me Mom, and I would be a major influencer of values and morals in addition to passing on living skills, beliefs, and ideals.

The reality of balancing a baby and a career set in when I returned to work after maternity leave. I had to deal with all the details of how to hold down the responsibilities of a career and raising a child. They all hit me straight in the face; it was serious business and now a human life was depending upon my husband and me. To keep my job, the decision to have our son go to daycare was an obvious solution as I continued to keep working at climbing the ladder of success and was determined to reach all my goals. I was not about to quit my job and stay home to raise our son.

To put children in daycare or stay home with them can be one of the most excruciating decisions parents make. Many times there are no options because of the financial situation and need for medical insurance, so using daycare is the answer. Every person will have their opinion on the subject of women working outside of the home or staying home to raise their children. It is an ongoing dilemma among women and we judge each other for our choices far too much.

As women, we are called to be mothers who are assigned the highly important role with significant responsibility in raising our children to imprint our values, traditions, and experiences on our children, our next generation. God does not want us to be pitted against each other on this subject of women working in or outside the home. One of the best approaches we can take is to try to understand each other more than criticize one another. The ultimate decision needs to be left up to God, the woman, her husband, and/or family to determine what's right.

> *Since this is the kind of life we have chosen, the life of the Spirit, let us make sure that we do not just hold it as an idea in our heads or a sentiment in our hearts, but work out its implications in every detail of our lives. That means we will not compare ourselves with each other as if one of us were better and another worse. We have far more interesting things to do with our lives. Each of us is an original.*
>
> GALATIANS 5:25-26 MSG

If we are truthful with ourselves and begin to focus on the reason why God values the faithfulness of mothers, we will begin to realize how pivotal it is for *every* woman to know that mothers have one of the most powerful and influential jobs on the earth. We as women must remember we are each different and uniquely created by God for His purpose. We are women who will continue to be strong and **worthy of our belief that women are a true creation and a gift from God that He highly treasures.** The endless qualities of a woman when they are coupled with the fear of God leads to honor, worth, success, and enjoyment. The following words say it so well. They are taken from an unknown Author and sum up so much that needs to be said about women.

Women have strengths that amaze men. We carry hardships and burdens. We hold happiness, love, and joy. We smile when we want to scream and can sing when we want to cry and cry when we are happy. We laugh when we are nervous. We fight for what we believe in and stand up for injustice. We don't take "no" for an answer when we believe there is a better solution. We go without so our family can have. We go to the doctor with a frightened friend. We love unconditionally. We are happy when we hear about a birth or a new marriage. Our hearts break when death crosses our path, yet we are strong when we think there is no strength left. We know a hug and kiss can heal a broken heart. All these qualities make us each so wonderfully made. We are internally beautiful and can outwardly shine with His light. Women have a mighty power of influence that will strengthen our children and hold the foundation of our homes solidly together until we stand in front of God and He says, "Well done my good and faithful servant."

After the birth of our second son which completed our family, and eighteen years in the corporate environment, God began to pull at my heart strings about the biblical responsibilities I had as a wife, mother, and woman. He clearly directed me to quit my job and stay home with our sons. It was not an easy decision and I wasn't even sure if it was God who whispered in a still, small voice. I rubbed my ears and wondered if they were plugged with the possibility that I misunderstood what I thought I heard and simply made it up in my mind. Pride nearly took over among my thoughts of being at home with no job to collect a paycheck. There would be no more important job title, urgent meetings to attend, the responsibilities of doing budgets, conducting employee interviews and evaluations, no more wearing or buying expensive clothes, and no more knowledge of the heartbeat of what was going on in the community. I didn't think I could do it. Would my years invested in a college degree, all my work experience, and the connections with people in the community all be gone? Maybe. I wondered if I was going crazy to make this move and would I be considered lazy? Who quits a great paying job at a solid company with good benefits to stay home?

I did quit my job that fully defined me for fourteen years to stay home with our sons. The choice to stay home to help them go through life has been the most rewarding job I've ever held. God changed my thinking by taking the skills He had given me to be successful in the corporate world and integrated them into parenting and managing our home. I gave myself a new job title: Vice President of

Hamilton Enterprises, a.k.a. wife and mom. A wife since 1987 and mother of one son in 1993 and the other in 1998.

The years I gave to corporate U.S.A. were a time of God stretching and molding me into the woman He wanted me to be. It was not an easy journey as I resisted many situations during those years. Yet they now are nuggets of wisdom and weigh little on the scale of who I really am. I wouldn't change the directions on this path as I gained knowledge and a strong understanding of the business world, made wonderful connections with many people, strengthened my work ethic, and developed sound business practices that I stand firmly on today. But the most noble and rewarding career I have had is the one of being a wife and mother. I've never received any tangible wages in dollar bills, yet all the time and energy that has been invested is the reward. Watching my sons mature and grow, to see successes, and some failures is now a new part of my role as a mom. Continuing to pray for them and being available when an ear is needed to listen is a lifetime assignment.

> *"For I know the plans I have for you," declares the Lord, "plans to prosper you and not to harm you, plans to give you hope and a future. Then you will call upon me and come and pray to me, and I will listen to you. You will seek me and find me when you seek me with all your heart."*
> JEREMIAH 29:11-13 NIV

I don't know if any of us will ever fully understand who we are to be when we grow up. God knows the plans for us, even though it seems like He reveals them slowly, sometimes bit by bit; it can be painful waiting. Being patient and praying for the answer to be revealed is the challenge because God works it out in His timing.

> But do not forget this one thing, dear friends: With the Lord a day is like a thousand years, and a thousand years are like a day. The Lord is not slow in keeping his promise, as some understand slowness. Instead he is patient with you, not wanting anyone to perish, but everyone to come to repentance.
>
> 2 PETER 3:8-9 NIV

We may not know the plan for our lives, but God does. We as women have a surplus of skills and talents that are phenomenal. Sharing them in our communities, work environments, churches, and families is great, but they also need to be intentionally shared with other women. Have you ever heard the phrase, "You need to be a Titus 2 woman"? Well, when I finally opened my ears to hear it, then read it for myself in the Bible, it took my breath away.

> Likewise, teach the older women to be reverent in the way they live, not to be slanderers or addicted to much wine, but to teach what is good. Then they can urge the younger women to love their husbands and children, to be self-controlled and pure, to be busy at home, to be kind, and to be subject to their husbands, so that no one will malign the word of God.
>
> TITUS 2:3-5 NIV

This scripture brought me to my knees in prayer for my insides to adjust to what God was asking of me as a woman. I have stumbled through my marriage because I continually would roll my eyes in disbelief to verses like this in the Bible. I would think, "You have to be kidding! Where in the world would there be women like this? There's no way I or any other woman in today's Americanized culture could be this type of woman."

The questioning continued: "This verse surely does not apply to women of current times? Or does it? Why would it not apply to us in this day and age?" My inquisitive mind has all kinds of answers. "Well, because it's old school and most women are not like this in today's world. Modern society tells women to have choices and freedoms to do as they please, to be leaders, to challenge society's current norms and standards, to push hard in the world, to be considered equal to whatever men can do, and to be strong enough to balance all the responsibilities women have on their plates."

For years I was baffled and hopeless in my internal desire to do ALL that God was asking me to do based on the content of this scripture. My belief was that IF I did decide to be this type of woman of God, He would have to turn me inside out, upside down, wash me, sew me back up, and make me look and act totally different! It seemed monumental if I were to become even a sliver of the woman described in these verses. There was no way it would happen, because I had too many hurdles to overcome and I was not sure of my willingness to give it one hundred percent.

I had to remind God that I was hard, harsh, and not so lovely of a woman, which I'm sure He already knew. The feelings of not being able to measure up to these requests put a heaviness of failure upon me. I pretended the scriptures didn't exist and whenever they were mentioned in any type of teaching or preaching, I'd look the other way emotionally with denial of ever being able to fulfill the request. But the verses kept on coming up in podcasts, conversations, and as I flipped through the Bible. Was it God pushing me to confront my weakness of self-examination in His definition of a woman? Yes. He knew I was ready to face my fears and inadequacies head on.

As the desire increased, I began to explore the verses. My heart was yearning with discovery, yet my mind was firing its rebellious arrows at what may be uncovered. I began with the perspective of finding a loophole in the verses which did not apply to women of today's era. I believed if ALL of it was true, change would be inevitable, there would be nothing left of the me that I knew. There had to be a way I could fit into this type of a woman and still be the real me. It was complicated in my mind and yet God knew how to minister to me by stirring up curiosity so I could learn and uncover more.

So the long and hard journey of studying this scripture began as I analyzed and prayed for understanding. There were more questions than answers for the longest time. How could there be women like this scripture described? Why would you want to be a woman like this? Why would I be obedient to my husband? Was I just good for keeping the home up and having children? These questions started as a way to prove myself right and find in the Word of God how it wouldn't work in today's age.

Why is acceptance of these verses so hard and negative for some of us? I believed if I took any of the words to heart, it meant I needed a total overhaul and it would be a lot of work, which would be too difficult and I would have to change too much. It also meant my belief system would have to be grounded in God more than the traditional system of our society.

I reminded myself that difficult scriptures do not have to be show stoppers. I was ready to dig into the Word to see what God wanted to teach me. My starting point was to dissect each word and examine it alone and how it applied within a section of the verse. This process can be slow, but it helps to make the verses come alive and allows for each word to become a nugget of gold when the words are clearly defined. It's like a treasure hunt—when you start you have no idea what you will find at the end.

Let's review the verses again before examining it thoroughly.

Likewise, teach the older women to be reverent in the way they live, not to be slanderers or addicted to much wine, but to teach what is good. Then they can urge the younger women to love their husbands and children, to be self-controlled and pure, to be busy at home, to be kind, and to be subject to their husbands, so that no one will malign the word of God.

TITUS 2:3-5 NIV

The two words I stumbled on that would make me fall flat on my face each time were "submissive" and "obedient." They have been complex words to inhale; even when trying to speak them aloud, they would make me gasp for air. I fought being what God truly wanted me to be and I knew pride was standing in my way with a defensive barrier of "woman hear me roar" and "get out of my way, or else." This thinking had to break. What was I so afraid of?

I was always a tomboy and not into many feminine things as I grew up. The tough exterior was my shield and any soft side of me was protected out of fear that someone would hurt me. I felt the gentle, caring side of me was weak, wimpy, and too emotional, as it proved to be in many situations. It made me feel vulnerable.

Yet, I had arrived at this turning point in my journey where finding my womanhood needed to be embraced. It was a process of accepting the fact that God only takes me down paths He needs me to go down. I need to warm up to ideas slower than most. The thinking goes like this: think about it, wait, think about it again, wait some more, then consider taking action. Do you get the picture? It comes down to...PROCRASTINATION!

In my heart I had a deep longing to change and become all God wanted me to be. I didn't want to continue to be labeled from my past. I had accepted God into my heart, was trusting Him on many things, and had instances of proof that He had not yet failed me. It came down to my willingness to be obedient to God. To honor Him with my willingness to have a different view and possible new behaviors.

So let's dive into the verses......

Likewise, teach the older women to be:

- **reverent**: Feeling or showing profound respect in the way they live.

- *not to be* **slanderers**: Words falsely spoken that damage the reputation of another, to not slander or attack someone's reputation.

- *or* **addicted** *to much wine*: Exhibiting a compulsive, chronic, physiological, or psychological need for a habit-forming substance, behavior, or activity.

- *but to* **teach** *what is good:* To cause to know something, to impart knowledge, to conduct instruction regularly.

- **Then**: Following next after, in order of position, narration, or enumeration.

- *they can* **urge**: To present, advocate, or demand earnestly or pressingly.

the younger women to...

This is a transitional point which moves me to review all that has been said to this point to make sure I understand before I move on. Once I can say yes, then I can work on what it's saying and the need to take action.

love their husbands and children,

Some of the visible things that we do to show love are keeping the house clean and presentable, making good meals, and keeping oneself in good health and condition. The unseen things to do are to continually pray, work behind the scenes on projects, and speaking positive words into others' lives.

to be self-controlled and pure,

- **Self-controlled**: The act of denying yourself; controlling your impulses.
- **Pure**: Free from harshness or roughness, free from moral fault or guilt.
- to be **busy**: Engaged in action, full of activity at home.
- to be **kind**: Of a sympathetic or helpful nature.
- and to be **subject**: As an adjective, owing obedience or allegiance to the power or dominion of another as to their husbands.

so *that no one will* malign *the word of God.*

- *so:* From that fact, reason, or as a result. This is what happens when you do all these things.
- *malign:* Speak unfavorably about.

This is another stopping point because it blocked me every single time I would read it. I had to take apart nearly every word and analyze the meaning. After tearing all of this apart, I need to restate the verse in a way which makes sense in my head. It sounds something like this: After choosing to do all the previous list of actions (love my husband and children, being self-controlled and pure, being busy, and kind), then I am to be subject (owing obedience or allegiance to the power) SO (doing all the listed actions) no one will malign (speak unfavorable about) the word of God.

Now is the time to stop again, PAUSE and think, ponder, and digest this packed full, meaningful scripture. There is so much information to be discovered that a break is needed to allow the significance of the word meanings to sink in. Then, we'll start again.

During this intense study which lasted for several years, God would encourage me along the way with His still, small voice. *This scripture is clearly spoken for how I want women to be yesterday, today, and tomorrow; a good wife and mom who is confident in her place in society.*

God made many things clear for me when I thought outside my intellect and core values. It was an exercise and test to think beyond my normal process of what was okay and comfortable in my personal world. The challenge is that we need to be open to the possibilities that our current reasoning may be limited and change may be required.

What I discovered was that I became more aware of what I believed God wanted for me as a woman—not you, just me. God does not want exact replicas of women walking around this world. One of each of us is enough! The scripture also gave me a greater understanding of other women and how God views all women. He has given us great responsibility and authority when we believe what He says and are willing to allow change to happen.

My negativity changed as I dug deep to study these verses. I was determined to become positive and believe God would reveal a profound meaning to get the understanding into my soul. I know He created me to be the woman who is in these verses, one who can live in our modern culture and be content. I have found my identity and feel comfortable with who God says I am, a daughter of the Most High, King of Kings, who loves me so much.

Twelve

Holding On to Let Go of Our Children

Innately I knew becoming a mother would change my world and it was going to be hard work. It would be a lifetime commitment with daily responsibility for eighteen years at a minimum. But, I finally wanted it. Once I conceded to my innermost self that I did want to be a mother, I was blessed to have children.

We have two sons that are five years apart in age and school years. This led to a feeling as if we had raised two only children. Not only in year separation was there a difference but also in their distinct personalities, with one being extremely self-sufficient and goal-oriented while the other was a free spirit and harder to get focused on anything, more of a social butterfly. This presented many obstacles in any parenting standards we thought we had figured out with the older son as they did not seem to work with the younger. They were vastly different and it played havoc on any set method we had devised as we navigated helping them get to adulthood. We continually prayed for trust and guidance that God could and would help us when He was sought.

When they were babies, I sat with each of them rocking in the early, quiet time of the morning when mother and child are totally still, gazing into my child's eyes to see the unique person God created. In my arms I was holding this tiny being who was perfectly made down to every specific detail. The deep love I felt was something I had never experienced before and was beyond my wildest dreams. There was a bond and connection unlike one my heart had ever experienced as we peered into each other's eyes. Holding them close I could smell their clean, fresh existence, and realized God was trusting me to influence their entire life. With my eyes shut and the aroma of a new baby, I would sing sweet words of hope and promises to them. I had fallen in love and knew I was meant to be the mother I thought I could never be.

The words I sang were prayers to God of gratitude for allowing and trusting us to raise these two boys. I did not want to let go of them or the moment as I dreamed of their life and what lay ahead: The friends they would make, the interests and activities in which they would enjoy and succeed, such as music, riding motorcycles, snowboarding, skate boarding, swimming. A mom's prayers for their future: school, friends, job, wife, and children.

I had them completely to myself and I did not want to let them go. Yet it was only a matter of time when I would begin to understand that God made mothers to be able to hold on and let go all at the same time. God gives mothers the deep understanding of holding on to let go, to be the trusted guide in their children's lives. The ones they come to for advice, to be the anchor when they have gone off course. From crawling to walking, walking to running, and the years of play dates and daycare friends, to elementary school and sports activities, to the awkward stage of preteen, to masculine teenager with the young man's voice that emerges along with facial hair that creeps on the scene, to the man who is securing his way in life, and then finding another woman who will take your place, to be the wife you prayed for and the one who will bring your grandchildren into this world.

There were many things my husband and I talked about before we had children that we would do intentionally as the boys grew. We believed in being available for them and being actively involved in their lives. We desired to implement traditional things like sitting at the table for meals to talk about our day, saying meal prayers, reading story books before bedtime, with prayers said to be instilled in their minds before drifting off to sleep, to attend their school and sports activities, to let them play musical instruments, to set rules and create consequences, and to always keep the line of communication open so they felt comfortable talking to us, and we to them, about anything.

And there were things we didn't discuss because we never thought about them. One of those was how education would play out in their lives. The older son was a good student, focused and self-disciplined, while the younger showed little interest in the education process. This led to a time when we considered homeschooling.

In the fall of 2006, God put a heaviness on my heart to consider homeschooling our boys, one in the sixth grade and the other in first grade. My initial response to this nudging was, "I must not have heard You (God) correctly. Did you say what I thought you said, homeschool the boys?" There was no way God would direct me—an extremely selfish, self-centered woman of the eighties "hear me roar" generation—to stay at home, with no other outside job to focus on, being a wife and homeschool mom. I must be downright crazy. I needed to pull the cotton out of my ears because the words I heard must have been muffled. There is NO way God could want me to homeschool the boys.

God had recently taken me out of my corporate career of fourteen plus years where I found my identity. I was proud of my ability to help our family financially and now that was not happening much, even though I had a few sideline businesses generating income. I personally felt less-than based on the world's perception of a career woman. It looked like many things were being stripped away from us financially. God was beginning a several year process in me to rely on and trust Him to fully take care of us.

The homeschooling idea needed serious prayer before moving forward. The idea was growing on me, yet the bigger concern was if my husband was receptive to the idea. I started to pray, "God, if this is really You, let it be confirmed in my heart and my husband's." "God let us see the door opening." "Show us through others that this is the right decision." "God let my husband bring the subject up in conversation." I also prayed for myself and what this commitment would require of me. Having peace of mind was going to be my confirmation.

Here's how the confirmation came: There was a radio ad on a local Christian station announcing an upcoming event open to families considering homeschooling. It was a time to come and ask questions, look at curriculum, and understand the process. I'd heard it over the airways enough times that it caught my attention. I began to pray, "God if you want this to happen, then do it through my husband and this event." Well, what do you know, one day my husband said, "I heard this ad on the radio about a homeschooling event; maybe you should go?" This was the confirmation of my husband's heart softening and the answer to prayer.

On August 22, 2007, we started homeschooling our younger son who was entering the third grade. Our older son remained in public school as an eighth grader. Huge amounts of fear crept in with the reality of the enormous responsibilities of influencing a young life, helping him grow and succeed. Several good and positive thoughts would be deleted by dread and old records spinning in my head: I wasn't smart enough to handle the process, there would be a lack of social interaction with others, and how would we determine if he was learning anything. The self-demoralizing thoughts were constant as the enemy wanted the plan to derail quickly.

It was a continual fight to keep negative thoughts out of my mind. Nuggets of creative ideas on how to communicate and break through our son's walls of indifference to learning were coming to me at the speed of light. They induced excitement within me and I knew I could do it with God's help. God was in every step of the homeschooling years. He did a work in me and our son along with our entire family. These years have been forever etched in our minds. Daily prayers to stand firm in God's Word were spoken out loud to build confidence in my son and me. Plus we prayed for boundaries to be set with the enemy to guard doubt, worry, and fear that would rush in during the course of the day. In prayer we would also ask for creative, fun, hands-on learning applications and the willing desire to learn to blossom.

The days turned to weeks and then years of pushing through and praying for our son's willingness to obey and his desire to learn. There would be days of complete emotional exhaustion followed by renewal in the morning. Saturating him with God's Word, readings of great historical principles, and engaging in mathematical challenges became a norm. Understanding his hands-on learning style and the need to work on releasing energy became a reward in our style of school. Teaching him everyday practical skills were some of the most memorable projects. We learned how to create Excel spreadsheets, use Word and Power Point to sell handmade goods to raise money to purchase a laptop computer, and bake yummy goodies to practice math knowledge. He was going to speaking events with me and sitting quietly in the audience, using proper manners like shaking people's hands, engaging in conversation with adults, and completing a book report on what I spoke about at the conference.

God was instructing me in countless lessons which were new to my fast-track, multi-tasking, get-it-done personality. I gained understanding about how to slow down my well-worn path of high pace, taking time to rest my brain from constantly thinking, and stopping to enjoy the journey with my son. I continued to find increased joy in teaching and discovering ways to engage learning in all aspects of our lives. I started to love this way of life. The need for me to lighten up on my rigid habits and thinking were becoming normal and this journey was becoming more worn in and comfortable.

For three school years, third through fifth grade, we were thriving in this way of living and learning together. The relationship between two strong-willed people was tested and challenged but it created endurance. We had deep emotional talks, long drives, and took nature walks to burn off pent up steam. We had ice cream for breakfast, prayed on our hands and knees for each of us to make it through the day, played volleyball (beach ball) in the living room to learn the globe, and made batches of chocolate chip cookies. We played bingo with the elderly, delivered Meals-on-Wheels, learned cursive, learned what a noun was, and even how to sew pillowcases. Days that will be forever in our memories.

As with all journeys, there comes a time when you meet a fork in the road. Our two path choices were to continue homeschooling or reenter public school at the junior high level. Just as I, the teacher, was feeling confident in the education process, the student was challenging me more than

I had ever been challenged. In my motivational speaking platforms, I could inspire others to make a decision within themselves to change a negative behavior into a positive attitude and live a more rewarding life. But I could not find the right formula to stimulate our son to stay on task with learning, much less get him to choose to cooperate with positive behaviors. Each day was turning into a battle with no positive results. By the time summer came, I was weak and worn out and gave up on the home education goal.

Failure in surrendering my will and giving up on homeschooling haunted me for several years, especially when the public school environment became a stage for the outgoing, charming personality of our preteen son. Academically he was ahead of the students in several subjects, but his deep need to show off and capture attention overrode the desire to stay focused on numbers, reading, and writing. For the next three years of junior high, I hated our decision to return him to public school. My outgoing disposition turned inward to solitude. I believed we made the wrong decision and I had completely failed our son. Depression nearly took me down, but God was there, as He always is, to pick me up, dust me off, and redirect my path.

The negative energy I had was redirected into a home cleaning business and the beginning of my writing career. I was alone with God all day cleaning and praying. The new isolation was a time I like to call "sitting on the shelf." It felt like I was a teacup and saucer that was set on a shelf, collecting dust, not knowing why I wasn't being used. Yet it was in the solitude, the praying, the

God time, and the physical work where God did so many amazing things in me.

> *So do not fear, for I am with you; do not be dismayed, for I am your God. I will strengthen you and help you; I will uphold you with my righteous right hand. For I am the Lord your God who takes hold of your right hand and says to you, 'Do not fear; I will help you.'*
>
> ISAIAH 41:10, 13 NIV

The other issue we, as new parents, never discussed was if we would take our children to church. We did. It was Sunday morning and we had arrived at church with a sigh of relief because we made it before the worship music started. I prayed over them to be on their best behavior so I could possibly listen to the sermon that day. So I was thrilled that the boys were fully engaged and there were smiles on their faces. The duration of one to two hours for church is a challenge for an antsy five-year-old who is pushing toy cars around his space within the boundaries of the aisle. The newborn son I was holding was quiet for the time. The main objective was to survive the time by making sure no toy cars went flying out into the aisles of chairs and the baby didn't start crying for the whole hour. I couldn't fathom when I would be able to engage in worship or sit quietly listening to the sermon with none of these distractions. According to older women the time with your young children goes by so fast and before you know it they are grown.

Now I'm the older woman and I agree with that statement as I sit in church somberly, quiet with my thoughts.

I'm captured by the worship music and hear every word of the sermon loud and clear. I can observe others around me and intently watch young moms with anxious looks on their faces, just like I had so many years ago. I realize how fast time passed and thank God for every moment He gave me with our sons. Even though they are now living their own lives, my job as a praying mother will never end, it changes, but never ends; it is my number one responsibility.

Praying for our children through their entire lives is what I was told to do by wiser, older women when I was a young, new mom. I didn't fully understand what it meant to learn to let go and let God protect them. Yet God directed me in how to pray for them. It was a prayer I said over them daily before they left the house, asking God to keep them healthy, safe, and strong; for favor in their daily activities; a hedge of protection to surround them from any evil schemes; and for God to be ever-present in their lives. No matter what they are going through I would pray without ceasing.

Always be joyful. Never stop praying. Be thankful in all circumstances, for this is God's will for you who belong to Christ Jesus.

1 THESSALONIANS 5:16-18 NLT

In the process of praying for the boys there have been days when I didn't want to pray, I didn't even want to give them a hug or say the words "I love you" or recite the prayer when they exited the house. It's challenging to stand by and watch your children make choices we may not agree with as it can be disheartening and frustrating. When this happens, the main objective is to capture all these negative thoughts and turn them into prayer, concentrating on knowing that God hears our prayers and He, not me, will do what needs to be done in their lives. God never told me how hard it was going to be, how I wouldn't want to talk to them some days, and how I would wonder if I was really made out to be a mother. Yet, I promised God I would never stop, even as they became grown men.

We destroy arguments and every lofty opinion raised against the knowledge of God, and take every thought captive to obey Christ.

2 CORINTHIANS 10:5 ESV

Over the years many prayers have been answered while others have not yet, as it is in God's timing. His timeline can never stop our prayers from being raised up to God every day. Now, as the years approach a new era of the hopes of grandchildren, it will also be another "holding on to let go" phase of life. There may be a time when it will come full circle as I sit as a grandmother holding my grandchild in my arms, smelling the sweet aroma of a baby, while looking in their eyes seeing God in them, and singing sweet prayers to them as I "hold on only to let go."

Prayer permeated my soul, it brought relief when I was agitated.

Thirteen

Reason to Pray

We need to pray to communicate with God, and when we do, it strengthens our relationship with Him and it releases are emotions, typically worry and fear. In the New Testament Jesus taught the disciples to pray.

> *One day Jesus was praying in a certain place. When he finished, one of his disciples said to him, "Lord, **teach us to pray**, just as John taught his disciples." He said to them, "When you pray, say: 'Father, hallowed be your name, your kingdom come. Give us each day our daily bread. Forgive us our sins, for we also forgive everyone who sins against us. And lead us not into temptation.'"*
>
> LUKE 11:1-4 NIV

According to the Webster's American 1828 Dictionary, *prayer* is earnestly asking for a favor by communicating to God. Additionally, it describes prayer in *worship*, a solemn address to a Supreme Being consisting of *adoration* or an expression of our sense of God's glorious perfections, *confession* of our sins, *supplication* for mercy and forgiveness, *intercession* for blessings on others, and *thanksgiving* or an expression of gratitude to God for His mercies and benefits. A *prayer*, however, may consist of a single petition, and it may be extemporaneous, written, or printed.

Working on our prayer life is similar to developing any habit we want in our lives, it takes practice. Developing dependence on lifting up our pure and honest desires of our heart to God with sincere words as we express ourselves in prayer is what God is looking for. It may not always be the words of praise and joy, it can be the frustrated and angry words, but know God has big shoulders and is able to listen to any words that need to be said.

The Psalms are full of prayers of many types: praises to God, thanksgiving, requests, sorrow, anger, confession, faith. Explore them for yourself to see that nothing that can be said to God is off limits. The following verses are a few from the book of Psalms:

The Lord is my rock, my fortress and my deliverer; my God is my rock, in whom I take refuge, my shield and the horn of my salvation, my stronghold.

PSALM 18:2 NIV

Be still before the Lord and wait patiently for him; do not fret when people succeed in their ways, when they carry out their wicked schemes.

PSALM 37:7 NIV

You hem me in behind and before, and you lay your hand upon me.

PSALM 139:5 NIV

Many of us are taught formal prayers to memorize when we are young, while some of us may never have had this experience. The first prayer I learned was the Serenity Prayer. Its author has been debated for years.

God, grant me the serenity to accept the things I cannot change, the courage to change the things I can, and the wisdom to know the difference.

In researching the background of the history and author of the Serenity Prayer, I found that it is based on a great scripture I like.

So do not fear, for I am with you; do not be dismayed, for I am your God. I will strengthen you and help you; I will uphold you with my righteous right hand.

ISAIAH 41:10 NIV

It was a huge accomplishment for me to memorize the Serenity Prayer as I had never had the desire, yet my willingness to change outweighed the ugly character defects I could see in myself. It was the beginning of realizing I was not in control and that God was. I used the prayer anytime I didn't know what to do, which was often. It began to roll off my tongue and was in my mind all the time. I was able to say it slowly and even stop at the breaking sections to ponder what each phrase meant. As this prayer permeated my soul, it brought relief when I was agitated, so that meant I said it a lot! As the time passed, I started to say it every time I went to the bathroom. It was during a time when the boys were young and it seemed as it was the only place where I could find a few minutes of quiet. In years to come this continued and it has now become an example I share when helping others learn how to step away, cool off, refocus, and pray—"Go to the bathroom and say the Serenity Prayer."

The next prayer I memorized was the Lord's Prayer, and as I mentioned already, it took much longer to get in my brain. It's traditionally said at the closing of a twelve-step meeting and during communion at church. It brings me comfort because it reminds me of Who is in charge of my daily needs, to forgive others, and to not be led into temptation.

The next challenge was to learn how to pray in a free flow format. It's like talking to a person, airing my requests, worries, and fears to God in every day words. This took time to get comfortable with as it seemed strange as if I were talking to myself. But, when I remembered that God is all around me, that He is the Holy Spirit that lives in me, I became more confident. Talking to God as He is my friend has been the key to enhancing my free flow prayers.

Once I felt comfortable with turning my requests to open prayer to God, the next thing was consciously praying for each of my family members and myself. For my immediate family, I took an index card and wrote prayers that were immediate in my heart and put a date on the card so I would be able to note how long it took to get an answer. Some of those prayers were answered quickly, some took years, while others have still not been answered. Saying daily prayers for myself was hard to do as it felt selfish. However, I was taught that I can and need to lift up my personal needs and desires to God so He can help me be the best person He wants me to be.

Believe that prayer works and begin to do it by finding prayers and verses which resonate with you. Work at memorizing them and getting them deep within you so they can be drawn upon when needed. Pray for your family members and yourself and see what God will do through the power of prayer.

Daily Self Prayers

Holy Spirit saturate me/us. Hover over us.

In a desert land he found him, in a barren and howling waste. He shielded him and cared for him; he guarded him as the apple of his eye, like an eagle that stirs up its nest and hovers over its young, that spreads its wings to catch them and carries them aloft. The LORD alone led him; no foreign god was with him.

DEUTERONOMY 32:10-12 NIV

Take all my thoughts captive.
I have the sound mind of Christ.

The weapons we fight with are not the weapons of the world. On the contrary, they have divine power to demolish strongholds. We demolish arguments and every pretension that sets itself up against the knowledge of God, and we take captive every thought to make it obedient to Christ. And we will be ready to punish every act of disobedience, once your obedience is complete.

2 CORINTHIANS 10:4-6 NIV

Bind any evil and generational curses in our presence.

...On each side of the river stood the tree of life, bearing twelve crops of fruit, yielding its fruit every month. And the leaves of the tree are for the healing of the nations. No longer will there be any curse. The throne of God and of the Lamb will be in the city, and his servants will serve him. They will see his face, and his name will be on their foreheads.

REVELATION 22:2-4 NIV

Bind my critical thinking; let confidence abide in me.

For we do not have a high priest who is unable to empathize with our weaknesses, but we have one who has been tempted in every way, just as we are—yet he did not sin. Let us then approach God's throne of grace with confidence, so that we may receive mercy and find grace to help us in our time of need.

HEBREWS 4:15-16 NIV

I am the head and not the tail, above and not beneath.

The LORD will make you the head, not the tail. If you pay attention to the commands of the LORD your God that I give you this day and carefully follow them, you will always be at the top, never at the bottom.

DEUTERONOMY 28:13 NIV

Put on God's armor and walk with it
in the fruit of the spirit—love, joy, peace,
patience, kindness, gentleness, and self-control.

Therefore put on the full armor of God, so that when the day of evil comes, you may be able to stand your ground, and after you have done everything, to stand. Stand firm then, with the belt of truth buckled around your waist, with the breastplate of righteousness in place, and with your feet fitted with the readiness that comes from the gospel of peace. In addition to all this, take up the shield of faith, with which you can extinguish all the flaming arrows of the evil one. Take the helmet of salvation and the sword of the Spirit, which is the word of God.

EPHESIANS 6:13-18 NIV

But the fruit of the Spirit is love, joy, peace, forbearance, kindness, goodness, faithfulness, gentleness and self-control. Against such things there is no law.

GALATIANS 5:22-23 NIV

LOVE and do for others
as I want done to me.

Do to others as you would have them do to you.

LUKE 6:31 NIV

Pray without ceasing.

Pray without ceasing.

1 THESSALONIANS 5:17 KJV

Show me visions and dreams.

In the last days, God says, I will pour out my Spirit on all people. Your sons and daughters will prophesy, your young men will see visions, your old men will dream dreams.

ACTS 2:17 NIV

Let contentment abide and raise me up.

You're blessed when you're content with just who you are—no more, no less. That's the moment you find yourselves proud owners of everything that can't be bought.

MATTHEW 5:5 MSG

I have worth and status in God's eyes and in my own.

I praise you because I am fearfully and wonderfully made; your works are wonderful, I know that full well.

PSALM 139:14 NIV

I am lovable and can love and have a tender heart!

Do everything in love.

1 CORINTHIANS 16:14 NIV

And be kind to one another, tenderhearted, forgiving one another, even as God in Christ forgave you.

EPHESIANS 4:32 NKJV

Give me tenderness to see the needs of others as You do.

But the Lord said to Samuel, "Do not look on his appearance or on the height of his stature, because I have rejected him. For the LORD *sees not as man sees: man looks on the outward appearance, but the* LORD *looks on the heart.*

1 SAMUEL 16:7 ESV

I pray for continued trust in our relationship, God—only in You and what You have planned. You (God) will fulfill your promises for me!

For I know the plans I have for you, declares the LORD, *plans to prosper you and not to harm you, plans to give you hope and a future.*

JEREMIAH 29:11 NIV

Let gossip not spew from my lips.

A gossip betrays a confidence, but a trustworthy person keeps a secret.

PROVERBS 11:13 NIV

Work with _____ (your husband), not against him. He loves me so much. Help him, and help me not to fight him.

Her husband has full confidence in her and lacks nothing of value.

PROVERBS 31:11 NIV

A joyful mother of spiritual children.

He gives the barren woman a home, making her the joyous mother of children. Praise the LORD!

PSALM 113:9 ESV

I will give ALL the glory back to God
for all He has allowed me to do.

So I commend the enjoyment of life, because there is noth-
ing better for a person under the sun than to eat and drink
and be glad. Then joy will accompany them in their toil
all the days of the life God has given them under the sun.
ECCLESIASTES 8:15 NIV

Fourteen

Chain Breaker Prayer

In the darkness of my past lifestyle, I felt as if I was in prison and unable to escape. I was held down with chains of shame, remorse, unforgiveness, and guilt about the way I lived, never feeling I would be set free. I was ready to let this way of living be the norm. BUT THEN God...

Each link in the chain represented feelings, ill behaviors, negative memories, harsh words said to me, worries, fears, anger, doubts, lies, confusion, along with generational baggage from those who came before me. Shackles confining me and preventing me from moving forward.

Once when I was listening to a Christian teaching about generational curses that are bound to us by our past family who we may have never known, a light went on in me. Some, if not a majority, of the heaviness I felt bound by could have been from the past generations. After this educational information, I began to actively pray that those troubles be removed and broken. It was important for me to pray that these issues of past generations not be carried on to my children or grandchildren. The specific phrasing I used in this prayer was, "Father break the generational curses that want to bind me."

Each of us bring family issues that can link together to form a chain to hold us down to those issues. Examples of the links are addiction, perversion, doubt, adultery, anxiety, mental illness, promiscuity, anger, over-eating, gambling, physical and/or sexual abuse, and when we marry, they are formed together with our mate and can be produced in our children. Well, I wanted to be the generation to stop the curses that have bound our family by letting God be the chain breaker.

> *Don't bow down and worship idols. I am the Lord your God, and I demand all your love. If you reject me, I will punish your families for three or four generations. But if you love me and obey my laws, I will be kind to your families for thousands of generations.*
>
> EXODUS 20: 5-6 CEV

Hearing these words from the Bible ignited my determination and discipline to say what is rightfully mine in God's kingdom. Being a committed person of prayer, I became willing to do what needed to be done to help my future generations. I am bound and determined to pray against the links in the chain that tend to hold us captive. The shackles must not hold us down. I pray for the exact opposite reaction for the link to be broken. The negative bondage that I sense, feel, or see is on one side of the column, while on the opposite side is the positive trait that is said to God in prayer, believing He will answer.

Chain Breaker Prayer Column

Shame ⇨ Respect

Guilt ⇨ Right standing/goodness

Worry ⇨ Peace

Fear ⇨ Trust

Pride ⇨ Humility

Anger ⇨ Compassion

Doubt ⇨ Faith

Lies ⇨ Truth

Confusion ⇨ Confidence

Hate ⇨ Love

Resentment ⇨ Kindness

Despair ⇨ Hope

Darkness ⇨ Light

Sadness ⇨ Joy

As a mom, I pray. As a wife, I pray. As a daughter, I pray. As a person, I pray. Praying is the only way to remove the obsession from my mind and loosen the things that want to bind me and my loved ones. My prayer regarding a lack of trust, for example, goes something like this: "Let go, I have no control, I need to let God flow." Or when perfection creeps in, I pray, "It is fear all tidy and looking fine and it cannot be mine." When procrastination stomps its way through my life, I pray, "It is another form of fear but this one is collecting dust and looking a mess, so get out of the way so I don't stress." If these links in the chain are not released with my prayers, I have to keep on praying and praying some more; eventually God will answer them.

Being set free from the weight of these torments can actually be felt. I am a witness to it as one who has been set free of many, if not all, of the harms that tried to hold me down. I've felt the links in the chain be loosened and broken so I know it works, and I need to keep praying for myself and my family. I believe when one can pray for themselves this is when God, the chain breaker, really comes into action for us. I prayed that my sons would not be bound by generational links, that they would not be captured by the chain. But some have bound them, and I know that my sons are the only ones who can work on freeing themselves when they set their minds to the love of God and His redeeming grace and begin to pray for themselves. When this step happens in our lives, we will never be held prisoner again.

For God will break the chains that bind his people and the whip that scourges them, just as he did when he destroyed the vast host of the Midianites by Gideon's little band.

ISAIAH 9:4 TLB

He brought them out of darkness, the utter darkness, and broke away the chains.

PSALM 107:14 NIV

Meal Time Prayer

Close to thirty years had passed since I set eyes on a woman I helped early on in her journey to find freedom from addictions. Over the years I wondered where she was, if she made it, and if she was happy, joyous, and free. Then one unusual day during a pandemic which struck our world, I was attending an online virtual meeting and my eyes were drawn to this woman who looked vaguely familiar. My eyes immediately went to her name and it matched the same young woman I met those many years before. It was her! And to my excitement she wanted to connect later to catch up on the many years that had passed. During our long visit to reminisce and catch up, she told me that any time she shares her personal story to freedom it includes a portion about me and something I gave her that has never left her memory.

We met when we both were new to finding ourselves and not wanting to be bound by addictions anymore. I shared my experience, which at the time was all of six months, about how to live a good life, one that included basic living skills. Being the encourager at heart, I can always pull hope out of others as I can see the good when they cannot see it themselves. I shared a tip I was currently using and very proud of, which was writing meals on index cards. I was newly married and had worked hard at writing every meal I knew how to make, about five, on an index card which I could refer to when I questioned, "What should I make for supper?" This was back before the Internet and the capability to search online for meal ideas. She was working on developing good habits of preparing and eating better and this was a novel idea she liked. Little did I know the significance this small idea would have on her until these many years later. The profoundness of it was extremely simple, sharing an idea that worked for me that may work for her.

Those well-worn index meal cards were the beginning of my love for cooking and making others happy through this skill. It has been therapy to me and a release of joy as I see others smile and express their enjoyment of the food. However, I didn't arrive there until I hit many pot-holes along the way. Busyness, life, and moving pushed those meal cards way in the back of a recipe box where they were long forgotten by the time I could have used them again. I was deeply into the frantic, fast-paced life-style and did not remember those handy index cards. My mind could only think of one thing as a young mom and it was what many of us say every day, "What do you want for supper?" Which is commonly followed with the reply, "I don't know." OR "Whatever you make is fine with me." To which another typical response will come, "Do you have any ideas?" And then the traditional last comeback, "No, whatever you decide to make is fine."

With eyes rolling in frustration, anxiety steaming out of me, I would frantically try to dream up the next delicious, TV cooking channel dish made in less than thirty minutes with five or fewer ingredients. Ugh! This conversation was a daily one for years when I had a full-time job with two young children. The ensuing discussion after the question and the same answers with slightly differing responses happened each night.

I had been busy at work all day and did not give any thought to what I would make for supper, even though it was a constant nagging whisper in my mind which I pushed farther back as the day progressed. Once I was off work I was agitated because I knew in less than a half-hour a meal plan needed to be implemented. The drive to daycare to pick up the boys was too short to orchestrate a nutritious meal. Maybe a billboard or a restaurant would trigger an idea. NOT!

Trying to be pleasant to the boys was a challenge when this annoying statement lingered, "What's for supper?" Hoping to find a wonderful meal idea, I'd ask the boys, "What did you have for lunch?" I needed to not sound desperate or duplicate the meal they had several hours earlier. Occasionally, an idea would strike me and I would be set, yet most times it was the kid-friendly basics like macaroni and cheese with hot dogs, which the boys would eat at every meal if they were allowed. My cooking skills had improved significantly over the years with crockpot meals, grilling outdoors, and freezer meals, but there were lags in my preparedness and it made me desperate more than ready.

Arriving at home, I became even more pressured and frustrated at myself. If my husband was home when we arrived, I would be like a cannon ready to explode, "Do you have any ideas for supper?" would be the first thing out of my mouth. There were no pleasantries of, "Hi, how was your day?" or "It was a busy day and I forgot to plan something for supper." It was the firing arrow question aimed at him to fix the problem I had created. Well, as most women know, the exact words I got back were, "NO!" Then the mental barrage of self-condemning statements would begin, "You knew you should have planned something this morning. You're so stupid. Now what are you going to do? It needs to be fast. Think of something."

This situation replayed each day with me hoping it would someday be different and somehow the food would magically appear and, tah dah, the meal would appear on the table. It tortured me mentally and I needed it to STOP. The lazy part of me was looking for the easy way out and the disciplined me knew I had the solution—meal planning. I know you've heard it a million times and many of you have done it before with varying degrees of success. It may have been for a short time and then you went back to the same old question, or it may have been the key of success to the haunting dilemma.

We all need to eat, and it traditionally is the responsibility of the woman of the household to prepare the meal. Of course, it can be different for some households but typically it's the woman who has this daily task. It is a daunting undertaking to continue to plan and prepare meal after meal, day after day, if we choose to eat at home.

Every prayer and positive attitude is needed to keep up with this difficult chore of meal prep as it continues during each stage of life. When children are small, the menu of items they like is narrow, and as they grow you'll make whatever they will eat even if the same meal is prepared three times a week. With teenagers in their active years, we seem to load them with carbs and lots of protein. As we move to the kids being gone, it's easy to revert to before-children habits of eating whatever you like or eating out at restaurants more often.

My mind was blank the majority of the time in regard to meals, and it seemed that nothing would spark any ideas so I began to resent the responsibility and anger would be my outburst. This needed to stop because there was nothing more that I wanted but to provide a meal-time experience sitting at the table with each other that was enjoyable. A time to thank God for the day and engage in conversation about the day's activities. I would try my very best and push through my frustrations, sit down with heavy shoulders wishing I could change something. Then before we ate, my husband would say a prayer, "Thank you God for this food, let it be nourishment to our bodies, and bless the maker of the food and everything she touches." Wow! My husband was praying for me each meal and I only heard it just then. God got my attention with this portion of the prayer. My negative attitude about meal planning dawned on me as God wanted me to get an attitude checkup with Him.

Soon after this awareness I was journaling during my quiet time with God; well, it was more like grumbling and complaining about this meal-preparing responsibility. I remember talking to God, "I know I need to make one or two meals every day. I get sick of doing it. I don't know what to make any more. I've run out of ideas. I need your help." There were no gourmet dish ideas that plopped into my head, but God gave me an idea; I was to take the mumbling and grumbling and turn it into a prayer—a Meal Prayer.

This Meal Prayer goes like this, "God, we have plenty of food in our home. Please help me create an idea for a meal today." It's short and to the point and I am excited to share with you that nine times out of ten within a brief time God drops an idea in my mind for a meal. I found a verse to be reminded that God will take care of ALL things when I stop the whining.

And day by day, attending the temple together and breaking bread in their homes, they received their food with glad and generous hearts.

ACTS 2:46 ESV

Each day I say this prayer early in the morning to help stop the frustration of being responsible for preparing oodles of meals. I've turned my once complaining, baffled thoughts of "What should I cook today?" to "I need your help God." This twist in thinking has resulted in more pleasant, stress-free days because I have released it to God and He directs me on what to make. It can be a simple or elaborate meal, it doesn't matter to me because it's an idea. Thank you, God, for helping me.

It doesn't matter your level of ability in the kitchen when the perplexing question of meal prep is turned over to God, because He will do in you what you cannot do for yourself. It is amazing to be a witness to what He will do within us and for those who will receive the end result. Plus, it's fun to see what ideas will flow and how the negative chore can turn into a time you look forward to because you know God is fully in the plan.

It's a
signal
to start
the day.

Sixteen

Getting Dressed Prayer

My mom taught me from a very young age that each day we needed to get out of our pajamas and get fully dressed even if we had no place to go. Once we were dressed, it was a signal to start the day. There were times when we never left the house, but it made us ready for whatever may happen in the day. Years later this applied to Christian teachings; the Bible reinforces this idea of getting dressed in the spiritual realm. So, while I'm getting dressed in the morning, using the verses' practical application referring to the Armor of God and each piece it represents empowers me spiritually to be ready for the day.

> *Be strong in the Lord and in his mighty power.* **Put on** *all of God's armor so that you will be able to* **stand firm** *against all strategies of the devil. For we are not fighting against flesh-and-blood enemies, but against evil rulers and authorities of the unseen world, against mighty powers in this dark world, and against evil spirits in the heavenly places. Therefore,* **put on** *every piece of God's armor so you will be able to resist the enemy in the time of evil. Then after the battle* **you will still be standing firm***.* **Stand** *your ground,* **putting on** *the belt of truth*

and the body armor of God's righteousness. For shoes,
***put on** the peace that comes from the Good News so that*
you will be fully prepared. In addition to all of these,
***hold up** the shield of faith to stop the fiery arrows of the*
*devil. **Put on** salvation as your helmet, and **take** the*
*sword of the Spirit, which is the word of God. **Pray** in the*
*Spirit at all times and on every occasion. **Stay alert** and*
be persistent in your prayers for all believers everywhere.

EPHESIANS 6:10-18 NLT

I'm told to PUT ON (an action word) God's armor so I can
STAND FIRM. The Armor of God is like putting on my
clothes when I get dressed in the morning. I don't go out
of the house naked. I must take action and PUT ON my
clothes so I can go out, STAND FIRM, to be ready for the
day. These action-packed words led me to a practical way
to remember each piece of the armor. The visual aspect
of learning helps me memorize and solidify verses in the
Bible that can help me live a good, practical lifestyle. Each
piece of the Armor of God is a weapon that allows me to
become a warrior in God's kingdom making me stronger
and wiser to the enemy's schemes so I can face whatever
comes my way.

God's Armor
PUT ON to STAND FIRM

Belt of Truth

In Biblical days the belt was like a girdle. I don't like gir-
dles—but I imagine it was a full body girdle. Picture it now

—squeezing yourself into one—I'm screaming with being uncomfortable. Or it can be a big, thick belt, one that hits right under the ribcage and goes to the belly button. These types of belts have gone in and out of style through the years, but they are great at holding in that flabby mid-section.

Shoes of Peace

These shoes cannot be flip flops. I visualize mud boots, the big goulashes type that go up to my knees. It prepares me for whatever may be out there to step in, because there are times in life when we get deep in doodoo and need to remain peaceful as we simply stand.

Breastplate of Righteousness

This is like the breastplate a knight in shining armor would wear: large, heavy, blocking any harm to come. The breastplate is only covering what is in front, so I like to make sure the back is covered with the

Robe of Righteousness

The robe can be visualized like a Batman cape, swishing and swirling so it can cover the back and front.

I delight greatly in the Lord; my soul rejoices in my God. For he has clothed me with garments of salvation and arrayed me in a robe of his righteousness, as a bridegroom adorns his head like a priest, and as a bride adorns herself with her jewels.

ISAIAH 61:10 NIV

TAKE UP
Taking action to shield my body.

Shield of Faith

This is a large, over-sized shield like the warriors of old used to protect themselves during battle.

Helmet of Salvation

This is no little peanut-sized helmet; this is a full-faced motorcycle helmet that covers everything.

Sword of the Word

The sword is a long, heavy, metal blade, being nearly six feet long. Yet I can lift it with no trouble as the weight is light in the Word of God.

FINAL REQUEST

Pray

In the Spirit on all occasions with all kinds of prayers.

Be Alert

Stay alert and be persistent.

It's an action-packed scripture which can profoundly impact a person's day when it is embedded in our memory. The action words of PUT ON, STAND FIRM, TAKE UP are ones to notice. Just like we take action with our physical pieces of clothing to get them on our body, it is the same with each piece of the Armor of God. Once we are dressed, we are prepared to take the final step: pray and stay alert. It is our responsibility as believers in God's army. Think of it this way: you wouldn't walk out of your house without your clothes on; neither can we walk out without our spiritual armor on. We are ready for the day!

Clean
and
PRAY.

Tisk Task, Go to Work

The trait of working hard is deeply embedded in me, so much that it can become a negative one at times when I place work above all else. Through the years I have leaned toward the tendency to be a workaholic as I can become obsessive about to-do lists and completing those projects and chores once they are on the list. Some call it obsessive-compulsive; however, I believe it keeps me organized, balanced, and not too lopsided in the quest of getting tasks completed. It has also been a method I've used to help alleviate swirling thoughts in my mind when worry tries to take over. Physical activity has always been a stress relief as it releases pent up energy from mental compulsions and bodily tension.

There has never been much idleness in me. I get this from my parents. It was instilled in me at a very young age that all of us needed to work hard and pitch in to help in whatever project we were doing. This strong work ethic was impressed upon us that there was no room for laziness. The reward when we worked hard was that we could play hard.

She watches over the affairs of her household and does not eat the bread of idleness.

PROVERBS 31: 27 NIV

I married into a family with similar ideals about work and play so my husband and I have continued to be hard workers. You will always find us staying busy with some sort of project. Our sons tell us we never rest. Well, once they left the house, we actually do sit way more than they ever saw us when they were living at home, but now we are a bit older and we get tired more easily. We want to keep busy and moving so we can live a long life. Staying active is the way we will accomplish it. We have a running list of things that need to be accomplished, and our sons know if they can't reach us on our phone that we are busy working. When they were young, we had to make a deal with them that we would stop all work projects at noontime during the weekend. This arrangement was negotiated after weeks of them complaining that all we did was work, work, work, and never played with them. Yikes, statements like that from the mouths of babes stopped us right in our tracks to evaluate our tendency to lean on the workaholic side.

The guidelines were established with each family member's input for when to stop and when adjustments needed to be made with the whole goal of making time for each other. We believe this trait is one we have carried on to our sons as they both show strong tendencies to work hard, yet place an importance on leaving room for play, fun, and rest.

Well, I could be done with this section and stop right there. NOT. Once I realized the need to be consciously aware of how much work we would do in a day or weekend, it became a subject matter that I took seriously. I needed to understand why work was placed on such a high level, learn how to stop when I really wanted to keep going, and think through the benefits that work gave me. My analytical brain shifted into high gear to begin the investigation.

I have placed work high above many other activities because I am good at it. When I work hard and I get results, that's the benefit. So the simple answer is I feel a sense of accomplishment. When I begin something, there is nothing there, and by the time I've spent a good amount of energy on it, *viola*, it has become something to enjoy. This is where more benefits come in; it relieves stress, things get thoroughly cleaned, and I pray during the project.

For several years after my corporate job was done, I started a home cleaning business and was blessed at the opportunity to clean for many families. Each week I cleaned their homes, I would pray for every member of the family along with my own family and myself. It was a quiet period of time that lasted for seven years. I questioned and resisted God when I wanted to be released from the work that was exhausting and put physical restraints on my body at times, but it was a season of growth in the area of releasing worry and learning to pray. I had become preoccupied with family members, their behaviors, and potential consequences. During my cleaning jobs, I would ponder and ponder some more—it was downright obsessive thinking, better known as worry. It went something like this…

Ponder things I wish I would have done differently.

Worry.

Wish I had made better word choices when I spoke in anger.

Worry.

Hope no harm was done by my hateful words.

Worry.

Question if the situation would have played out differently if another choice had been made.

Worry.

These self-doubting faults replayed in my mind and served no good purpose; they only tore my self-worth to shreds. It was mentally exhausting and made me physically tired. Yet I knew what the fix was for the out of control worry problem—keep physically working: scrubbing deeper, rubbing the dirt to a crystal clean glimmer, and working in a rigorous motion of wax on, wax off. I'd make the worry go away! Yet no amount of scrubbing and rubbing made the worry thoughts leave my mind.

One day as I dragged myself to a cleaning job where I knew I would need a lot of motivation for the next six hours, I decided a great way to kick start my lack of enthusiasm would be to listen to a podcast. I don't recall the title or the Christian speaker's name, but I remember the message: we need to take control of our thoughts by turning them into prayers. This statement hit me like a ton of bricks because I knew I was not practicing this. The Holy Spirit came upon me so heavily that I dropped to my knees in the living room of the house and cried to God,

"Help me take the worry thoughts away and help me be set free." This is when I heard a still, small voice with a simple phrase, "Clean and PRAY."

Clean and PRAY.

Clean and PRAY.

Clean and PRAY.

These three words saved my life from endless worry as I began to repeat them each time I cleaned. As I entered a house I would say, "Clean and pray, clean and pray." With every room, each hour, and every stroke of movement I would say, "Clean and pray." Every thought of worry was captured, restricted, and dragged to its death by a prayer.

It was a discipline of catching myself in the negative worry thoughts, then capturing each one by converting it to prayer. I would not let the enemy take hold of my mind, instead I focused on entrapping the negative, spiraling thoughts, and turning them over to God. It took a concentrated effort to redirect my thoughts when worry came in. It's cunning how fast a simple thought can take off down a bunny trail to explicit thoughts of devastation, projecting years into the future, with unrealistic results that may never happen. Crazy thinking, anxious thinking, worried thinking.

The Bible teaches us to not be anxious about anything, which seems next to impossible when we are in the height of the crisis situation. But our minds are power-ful, and when there is a focused effort to work on getting the Word of God into our minds instead of worry, great results will happen.

Don't worry about anything; instead, pray about everything. Tell God what you need, and thank Him for all He has done. Then you will experience God's peace, which exceeds anything we can understand. His peace will guard your hearts and minds as you live in Christ Jesus.

PHILIPPIANS 4:6-7 NLT

In the same way, the Spirit helps us in our weakness. We do not know what we ought to pray for, but the Spirit himself intercedes for us through wordless groans. And he who searches our hearts knows the mind of the Spirit, because the Spirit intercedes for God's people in accordance with the will of God.

ROMANS 8:26-27 NIV

God wants us to enjoy our journey in life, to be free of worry and to have peace and contentment, trusting He will take care of our burdens. Our time here on earth is to find enjoyment and not misery. I've said this before and will say it again, "It's easier said than done." So how do we get to this joy, peace, and contentment with our worries being turned over to God in prayer? Do more work.

In this analyzing of the work idea, I've realized that cleaning is my way of dealing with the mental and physical energy that wants to spin out of control. But what if you don't like to clean? Figure out what works for you. I know it's wise to have a list of things to do when our minds get into that crazy thinking—it's the go-to list of a variety of projects. I've categorized them into types depending on the amount of time and attention they take. It can be extremely helpful as it can help categorize the projects to make them more manageable to complete them and to give you the list on paper to grab when you need to distract your mind.

Four Types of Work Projects

Massive
A work load which takes more than a few days and/or additional people to complete. Example: stain deck, paint house, build a retaining wall.

Weekly
Able to accomplish within the same week. Example: pay bills, mow lawn, clean house or garage.

Daily
Complete within one day. Example: clean house, buy groceries, bake cookies.

Do On a Rainy Day
Classified as ones no one wants to do. Example: organize a junk drawer, clean the linen closet, dust ceiling fans.

Each type of project takes a different level of focus to complete, internal motivation, and a lot of prayer. In the learning curve of my journey, I have experienced the need for Massive or Rainy Day Projects to help me work through mental weariness or worry. It allows my active mind to focus on the physical activity of the project and the stamina needed, rather than sit idly and continue to obsess about the issue. This releases the tension in the physical body and reduces the mental energy that has been working overtime with the issue.

The other benefit of the four types of work projects is it allows for the making of lists. I love lists! Some of you are laughing because you are with me on the list-making. The rest of you are rolling your eyes because you despise the list-making people. Capturing my random project ideas on sticky notes is my way of doing it; they are located randomly around our home. Then they are rewritten on a legal pad of paper under the four types of projects with the goal of crossing them off. The crossing off is the finale and the end of the race for that task. A victory!

This is all in attempt to gain more peace and contentment by relieving my brain from swirling thoughts which create anxiety. God desires for us to walk the journey of life with Him hand in hand, strolling, not running off into the trees getting lost while He stands still waiting for us to return to Him. He waits patiently for us to receive the peace He has granted us once we still ourselves of the many thoughts and plans we have created. So the releasing on paper takes the overrun thoughts and allows them to be saved and allows God to help organize them so that we can gain freedom of the mind.

Having peace of mind is one of my highest goals to strive for in my life. Once I've experienced it, I want more of it. It gives me steadiness and ease throughout the day while allowing me to realize God is going before me, He is beside me holding my right hand, and behind me protecting me from the enemy's schemes.

As God has said to me, "*Let go, Let go, so I can FLOW.*"

God cares for you, so turn all your worries over to him.

1 PETER 5:7 CEV

In all your ways acknowledge him, and he will make your paths straight.

PROVERBS 3:6 NIV

I've learned
to put this
busyness to
better use.

Be Still to
Keep Moving

For those of us who remember when cartoons were available to watch on TV only on Saturday mornings, put your memory cap on.

Jumping out of bed, racing to be the first one to the TV, because if you got to turn it on first, then you were the one who ruled over what cartoon would be watched. Many Saturdays I got to be the controller. I'd grab my blanket and hope Mom would say it was okay to have breakfast in the living room. Breakfast consisted of toast with chunky peanut butter and grape jelly or a bowl of Cheerios with ice cold milk. I'd be set for the morning.

Settling myself down on the couch, I was ready to hear my favorite cartoon theme song from Bugs Bunny.

Overture, curtains, lights,
This is it, the night of nights
No more rehearsing and nursing a part
We know every part by heart
Overture, curtains, lights
This is it, you'll hit the heights

And oh what heights we'll hit
On with the show this is it!

When the music ended, I waited with high anticipation as they would play my favorite episode with Bugs Bunny and the Tasmanian Devil Taz. Taz would swirl around like a tornado and stop on a dime to mumble some incoherent words...blah, blah, blah. I'm not quite sure why I had an attraction to this ugly-looking character. It was fascinating to watch his spinning and twirling. I was glued to where he'd whirl off on his next adventure.

I have continually related to Taz's swirling, spinning, and stopping on a dime actions because I've been moving and spiraling like that since I was born. During all my years of school—elementary, high school, and college—I needed to be totally engaged in the topic for stillness to overcome me. It's part of my personality and who I am. The lack of being still has been a productive quality because I get many things accomplished. From the opposite perspective, not being still in my physical body leads to a lot of motion in my mind. My thoughts go as fast as my body and it takes me on what I call Bunny Trails or I could refer to them as Tasmanian Devil paths. I go from here and there, then back to there, wondering where here started.

I've learned to put this busyness to better use by engaging in formal exercise and by steering it towards completing projects. The art of quieting my mind is an acquired skill which has taken years to implement. Being still enough to hear my surroundings is a huge challenge. Here, you try it...be still and open your ears. What did you hear? Tick,

tick, click, click, chirp, chirp, the clock, the dog walking across the floor, the birds outside. These are all sounds to hear as quietness makes for stillness.

Being still is a quality God wants us to have so we can hear His still, small voice and hear the directions we need to take for our day. I have had to consciously choose to make stillness a part of each day and it begins with a few simple steps: sitting quietly for one to three minutes. Just sit still, that's it. As you work at it, it will become a well-formed habit and you will gain what the scriptures say.

Be still and know I am God.

PSALM 46:10 NIV

Let go [of your concerns] then you will know that I am God.

PSALM 46:10 GW

Do not be anxious about anything, but in everything, by prayer and petition, with thanksgiving, present your requests to God. And the peace of God, which transcends all understanding, will guard your hearts and your minds in Christ Jesus.

PHILIPPIANS 4:6-7 NIV

Three Things Gained by Practicing Stillness

Personal Insight

Things within you that need focus will come alive and you'll gain insight into what you need to do for the day.

Connection with God

The stillness brings enough quiet for God to connect with us, to help focus on the day.

Peace Within

The stillness is peace. There is quiet acceptance in being okay just where God has you.

Once I've practiced stillness, the direction for my day comes easily and my focus is given to me. It then becomes a habit that once my thoughts spin out of control, I can curtail them with stillness.

Never Stop Moving

"Keep moving or otherwise you won't be able to." This was a statement my mother-in-law said often in her last years. It constantly stays with me as a challenge to always keep moving my body with activities and regular exercise because if I don't, I won't be able to keep moving as I age.

Being a woman growing up in the 1980s, my first exposure to what the world now knows as individual exercise programs was of Jane Fonda in her skin tight leotard and leg warmers. She did flexible moves that only the cheerleaders and dancers were capable of doing, and she encouraged you to do the same, yet it seemed impossible. I was from the era that our exercise clothes in gym class were a well-worn t-shirt, short shorts, and knee-high tube socks, in addition to a good pair of flat soled Converse shoes. During this time other name brand athletic footwear was entering the market and every teenager was trying to convince parents to buy them a new pair for $25.00, which was a huge amount to spend on one pair of shoes when you compared it to the ones we wore at $5.00 a pair.

In high school I was active in basketball for a short time until I realized I had to understand and memorize the plays; I just thought it was getting the ball from the other person and making the basket. I was also in track every spring. But what I enjoyed the most was being a cheerleader because I was able to yell and be active. I liked using my loud mouth in a productive way by cheering on the team, but more likely annoying many people with the intense volume that came from deep within me.

During my college years there was no formal exercising; it was more about partying, eating whatever I wanted, and enjoying the freedom of living on my own until I gained thirty pounds my freshman year. When this happened, I knew it was time to figure out that the lack of activity was going to be detrimental to me if I continued on the path of bad eating habits, drinking alcohol, smoking cigarettes, and sitting around. During this time is when the concept of exercise equipment in a club environment started. Everyone was doing it so I wanted to do it too. I loved it. I thrived in the setting and saw great results by getting my weight under control, which helped me think differently about staying active and making it part of my lifestyle.

During the years I had babies, exercise went in a different direction. While I tried to keep going to a club, it worked against me mentally; it was too stressful trying to figure out when to fit it into the day. Going out to exercise was not working anymore, so I had to make the decision to stay home. This began a journey of buying VHS tapes, then DVDs, and now online access to my favorite type of exercise program that I continue to this day.

Ever since I was young, I have dealt with being chunky and have a difficult time keeping my weight stable. The problem is that I love food, cooking, and eating! I've had to like exercise as much as I love food, otherwise the added weight becomes a problem and I expand. Once the expansion happens, it affects my mental state of mind. The number on the scale has been an enemy as my obsessive thought process kicks in and I begin weighing myself daily. I'm fine with all of it when the numbers are in my favor, but once it goes in the other direction, I tend to sabotage myself with an 'I give up' attitude. I've gone so far as getting rid of the scale when the numbers have not been where they need to be and simply using my jeans as an indicator of success or failure. The last time I did this it was not good as I gained in excess of thirty pounds.

In my thirties I could eat whatever I wanted, exercise, and keep things under control. During my forties is when the reality of eating whatever I wanted began to hit my thighs. The five to ten pounds would not come off even when additional exercise was added. Then my fifties happened. Mentally I was embracing being a more mature woman who had come a long way in most areas in my journey of life. However, this is when I had to change my thinking pattern and focus on my WHY. My why in my eating and exercising choices is for health reasons. It cannot be about the number on the scale, and even though it's nice to see a more desirable one, it had to be about staying healthy for the last half of my life. I did purchase a scale again and worked at stepping on it once a week. I use an app on my phone to track my food choices and it helps me stay accountable to myself.

My current focus in exercise is to simply keep moving. Being honest with my family and friends is the key to success, because then they know my intention, my why, about enjoying food and continuing to move. The theory from my thirties of eating what I want and exercising to keep my weight reasonable is still a focus, but I've had to change my habit of eating too many sweets and traditional carbs. I love to cook, bake, and eat good food so it needs to be in moderation, not excess.

I have come to realize that eating in a balanced way and keeping my body active is for the rest of my life, not just for a certain amount of years and then I can quit and do whatever I want. This awareness has made me think in terms of the long haul and make adjustments along the way so success will continue. It has to become a program that works for me and something I would not give up on easily.

Personally, I get bored fast with an exercise routine that is constantly the same. So I have decided that movement must happen no matter what form it takes, but it must continue or, as my mother-in-law said, "Keep moving, otherwise you won't be able to move." By working at this way of life for many years, it has now become a lifestyle, not a 'have to.' I have several tips that can be helpful in making this a focus for life.

Tips for Making Exercise a Life Long Habit

Mentally Prepare Yourself

The night before, think about what exercise activity you'll do the next morning.

Get Out of Bed

When the alarm goes off, thank God you're alive and get out of bed. If snoozing is a habit, decide how many snoozes are too many.

Grab Your Exercise Clothes

On the way to the bathroom grab your exercise clothes and as you sit on the toilet change into them. Now, you're committed to go move your body in some form for at least thirty minutes.

Exercise for 30-45 Minutes

Monday through Friday set a goal to do traditional exercising in the morning. On the weekend find other activities to do so the pattern will be changed up and boredom won't set in. Pick what works for you whether it may be outside, at a gym, or inside your home, just move and do something.

Once these exercise challenges are met, I've learned to keep the flow going by continuing with a few more key tasks to keep a good, solid start for a successful day.

Keys to a Successful Day

Shower and Get Ready

Simple, yes, but one that can make the difference in your day. Whether you work outside the home or in, decide to get fully dressed and look your best regardless of whom will see you during the day. Do it for yourself. Remember we represent God.

Drink Plenty of Water

To keep a healthy body, it needs enough water to keep it alive. A standard formula for how many ounces of water to drink per day is to take your body weight and divide it in half. This number equals the amount of ounces of water to be consumed on a daily basis. A secret to success to achieve this goal is to try to drink two containers of water before you take a shower. Drinking one before you exercise to give your body the needed energy and the second round of water right after you've completed exercising. When you drink this water, imagine that you are giving your internal body a shower with the water you drink; it makes it much easier to consume.

Eat Smart

Starting the first meal of the day with a good breakfast that has some type of protein in it will be a good anchor for the rest of the day. A great idea to help make wise choices is to plan your meals for lunch and dinner when possible. Focus on a lunch with a light salad, sandwich, or soup. When snack time comes be ready with healthy options so you won't be swayed to negative choices. Snack on fruit, crunchy veggies, nuts, pretzels, or yogurt. Finish the day with a planned out supper that is balanced with a protein of your choice, vegetables, and a small portion of some type of carb.

Stretch Breaks

Take breaks for your body to stretch—I call them Thankful Breaks—every 45 minutes to an hour. Find apps on your phone or desktop and set notifications that pop up to remind you to take a break.

Shut Your Eyes

Yes, and if you work from home, take a 15-minute nap. It's not a full-out, snoring kind of nap, just a cat nap to rest your eyes and body from constant motion. Those working in a traditional office setting can find a quiet place like your vehicle if it's not below zero weather, or a single stall bathroom. Even five minutes of closing your eyes can help.

Sleep Well

Nightly sleep needs to be at least six to seven hours each day. Going to bed at approximately the same time is a good habit and one we need to remember worked well for our children, so we need to do it too.

Bonus Exercise

Additional exercise throughout the day is another great goal to try to achieve. Set out for a certain amount of steps per day so it is a challenge, or find an accountability partner to compare notes with and keep each other encouraged.

The ultimate goal—keep moving.

Dear friend, I hope all is well with you and that you are as healthy in body as you are strong in spirit.

3 JOHN 1:2 NLT

Fun Times

In the summer when I was a young girl, we were busy on the farm and had little time to have much fun. We'd be lucky if we got to go to the county fair for one day during the busy summer work. However, Dad liked to go to the state fair, and I do have many fond memories as we would take a well-deserved break from the farm work. During the years when we did not get to go, Dad had an interesting perspective on how to have our own kind of fun.

The times when the fair rolled around, my brothers and I would be excited to see if we could convince Dad and Mom to go, with hopes to go on the rides, eat some yummy food, and maybe play a carnival game. One summer when it was too busy to take the day off to go, Dad created his own carnival ride for my brother and me. Now remember this was in the 1970s, so safety will not be part of this story. Dad had an old Massey Ferguson tractor used mostly as a workhorse, yet it was reliable and used for many different purposes. It had an open cab and a large shovel bucket on the front end which measured about six feet wide, three feet deep, and about the same in height. In the center of the bucket was a metal stabilizing bar measuring about two inches in circumference. It was attached to the top and bottom of the bucket. Dad's solution for his whiny kids who wanted to go to the fair and go on rides was simple; he said, "Get in the bucket of the tractor and I'll give you a ride!" My brother and I jumped in as fast as Dad said it because we knew he'd act fast and he'd give us a fun time.

Not knowing what to expect, my brother and I hunkered down in the small of the bucket and were ready as we held on tight to the metal bar. Just like on a fair ride, we heard, "Hang on, this is going to be fun." He started the tractor and slowly lifted the bucket high in the air, then gradually brought it down, next we'd be moving in circles, then stop and turn back in the opposite direction. The whirling and turning was mixed with the bucket lifting up and down at the same time. I'm sure you could hear us squealing from a distance because we were having the time of our lives. And, just like a fair ride, you never wanted it to end, but it came to a stop. When it was done and we were safely out of the bucket with the tractor shut off, Dad came strutting over to say, "Now that's a fair ride you'll never forget." And, I never have forgotten it.

Fun as defined by Webster is what produces amusement or enjoyment, a mood for finding or making amusement. Being raised by parents with a strong work ethic and little emphasis on relaxing, having fun, or finding the joyful part of life, I know all too well how to work versus how to have fun. It has been a negative attribute of mine that seems to be a problem more than an asset.

As I grew up and left home, this focus of working more than having fun stayed a theme because having too much fun seemed like playing hooky, and if I was caught I'd be in trouble. When I started dating my husband, we did many fun things that were foreign to me, like fishing, golf, camping, riding a motorcycle. After we married, we continued to do several of these fun activities along with hard work. He was also raised by parents who believed in working hard first. Today, the way my husband and I have fun and relax tends to be uniquely different than most people we know. Our way of enjoyment revolves around finding excitement in a work project being complete more than the traditional definition of fun. We like to take a task that we know nothing about and then we set out to learn, work, and struggle to come to the end result of a completed task.

If you ask our sons about us having fun, I suspect they will roll their eyes and say, "Yeah, right." When they were young, they finally confronted us about how much work we did when we went to our lake cabin every weekend; we were out of balance. We told them we would have fun and go for a pontoon ride or ride a jet ski or sit and watch them play in the water or on the beach, yet by mid-afternoon we would still be working on a project that seemed to have no end time, and they would be very disappointed. As they bravely said, "All you guys do is work and don't want to have any fun." We had to stop! This is when we struck a bargain with them and ourselves that we would work until noon and then take the rest of the afternoon to have fun and enjoy the lake and them. Our boys still bring up this story when they call to ask what we're doing, working or having fun? Now, we have to be accountable to each other to take only a portion of the day for work and the remainder of it for rest and relaxation.

What does someone like me have to say about fun? Well, I'm a little stumped as to why God nudged me to write about it too, so much that I wanted to delete the entire section because I didn't have a lot to say in the traditional sense of the subject. There again is the theme that my books don't seem to follow the norm, but I just say what I do know because someone out there must be similar to me and needs to hear it.

It's been a process to redefine what fun and enjoyment means to me. Living by example is my best lesson, and I have been known to take things to the extremes in the process of finding the answer in the lesson. I know about the statement, "The truth hurts." When I am ready to learn the lesson God has for me in an area of my life, I know I must brace myself. I can't seem to let it be totally God's way; oh no, I tend to think I know better and try to work on it myself. I'll solve it before God does and then I will be successful. Okay, are you laughing yet? I am. My experience is that I will go from one extreme to the other; it defines me, like a clock pendulum, from one side to the other, black or white, right or wrong. In the area of fun, I have not gone to the extremes and had too much fun! Are some of you laughing? Stop! I know this is a weakness and I still need help in this area.

Learning to accept fun as a necessary part of life has been a process. I'd rather redefine fun as learning to have more JOY in my life. Once again using Webster for a foundation of understanding words, it says this about joy:

JOY:

- The emotion evoked by well-being, success, or good fortune, or by the prospect of possessing what one desires

- A state of happiness

- A source or cause of delight

The Lord is my strength and my shield; my heart trusts in him, and he helps me. My heart leaps for joy, and with my song I praise him.

PSALM 28:7 NIV

To keep it simple and in perspective, I have come to accept the JOY in my life. It is not the usual way to think of a fun time, like a long-awaited trip to a tropical island or a day-long spa treatment. Even though I have done these more traditional forms of fun and enjoyed them tremendously, it isn't my first thought when I think of fun. The way I've approached the need to have more joy is to listen to what God is saying for my style of fun. That includes things like working on projects that engulf my soul and fill me with excitement, or resting in the peace that overcomes my spirit when I experience an *aha* moment in nature. The key element is to be still enough in God's presence to learn what brings joy and fun inside of me. This challenge has been intense as the enemy tries to bring self-condemnation to the work God is doing in me as I simply try to sit still to find that quiet. This simple approach to my style of fun means slowing myself in the busy activity, being still to pause and breath, which brings the quiet and rest.

Nature has been my classroom to force stillness into my busy self. It is one of the single most captivating playgrounds that gets me to halt my active body into a statue to watch what God has set right before my eyes. Catching a monarch butterfly on a lilac bush to see the magnificent colors patterned so beautifully by the Designer himself is clearly breath-taking. My busyness comes to a complete standstill with mysteries that God only understands. Allowing a person like me to freeze in my activity to watch for a brief second what God has made in this world for me to enjoy gives me rest and joy, my definition of fun.

The subtle opportunities God has provided in my walk of learning about fun and joy have been amazing. They have spoken to my heart and stilled me enough to change my actions. I have gained the appreciation of the simple views in nature which have allowed me to realize this is what makes my heart skip a beat. At these times God has my attention and I've begun to understand the concept of slowing down, resting in His goodness so to refresh my soul.

Yes, my soul, find rest in God; my hope comes from him.
PSALM 62:5 NIV

The ultimate lesson is to rest enough to have God infiltrate my weakness with His will so change can occur and then my unique way to have fun and joy can come out. To find this REST, God gave me an acronym to remind myself of how to rest so my body, mind, and soul can be refreshed.

How To Find Rest

R—Relax, don't run, retreat from busyness

E—Easy does it, enjoy everything, be effortless

S—Sit, sing, seek, sleep

T—Take time, trust, tuck away truths

Come to me, all you who are weary and burdened, and I will give you rest.

MATTHEW 11: 28 NIV

I turn to
cooking
and baking
when my
mind feels
a mess.

Food Therapy

The door opens and the boys come rushing in from school to one of their favorite smells...fresh-baked chocolate chip cookies. They drop their backpacks, head for the sink to wash their hands, and immediately grab a fistful of warm cookies, a glass of milk, and drop themselves into a chair to devour the baked treat. As a mom, the smile is huge with pleasure to see how much they love the cookies that I worked hard at making for them to enjoy. This hard work is what I call my therapy and it has produced many good results and is a good way for me to work out the craziness in my head.

I turn to cooking and baking when my mind feels like a mess and I can't seem to straighten it out. It has been a way to release the pent-up emotions of the day. When some would walk away from the thought of cooking or baking as a form of release, I immersed myself in it. This has had positive and negative effects on others and myself. For others it has brought a ton of joy as the recipients of the great end result which is amazing food. For myself it has been negative at times because I have eaten my way to chubby results, yet have released lots of pent up feelings along the way as I baked my way through the emotions.

The picture of the process looks like this...apron goes on, all the items needed are pulled out of the cupboards along with my favorite recipe book chock-full of well-used favorites. The action and mess begin: scooping, measuring, chopping, leveling, peeling, kneading, mixing, spilling, wiping, tasting. With a large kitchen it gets more hectic as the space allows for items to be placed here and there and everywhere. And my theory is if you have a mess you may as well make a huge mess, so I rarely make just one item. Typically it will be several items in addition to an entire meal, all at one time.

The crazy cooking action is a picture of how my head feels a big huge mess with no rhyme or reason. Each thought tangled up with the other in hope that it measures correctly to make an amazing dish that will look wonderful at the end. While I'm in the process of this chaos, it seems like nothing is going to turn out because it's a confusing mess. Yet the end result is an amazing smell and an excellent-tasting food as the kitchen is clean and organized like nothing ever happened. All the ingredients, dishes, and kitchen are back to the original condition and it looks perfectly normal. Just like me. This is a laugh-out-loud moment, because I'm kidding.

I don't know why this works for me, but it does. It's some sort of distraction from what is happening in myself so I can concentrate and pray for myself and others. The products I make are gifts to those who receive them. It also is part of being in control of what looks like nothing to a wonderful and tasty dish. By the time I'm finished, I'm exhausted and the issues that were consuming my mind are gone. That's what I call effective therapy.

Over the years of using this remedy with tons of practice, I have used many recipes with some great successes along with a few epic failures. Those you can ask my family about as I know they will give you a few memorable examples. I have gathered a vast number of recipes from many different sources: my favorites, my mother-in-law, sister-in-law, good friends, and of course online searches. Some of these recipes have been tweaked in some way from their original formula or stand as they were handed down to me. They are some of my favorites and ones that are a constant stand-by, recipes that I'm known for making —signature items.

See Recipes from Sue on page 211.

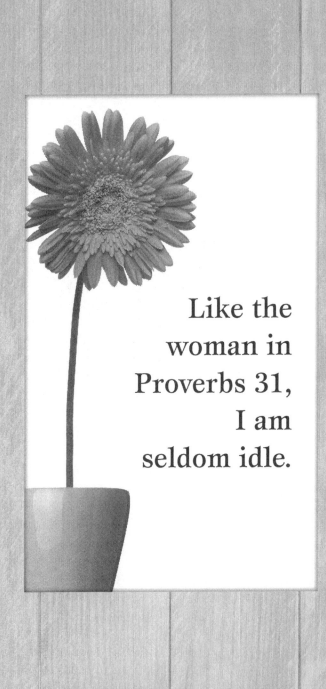

Like the
woman in
Proverbs 31,
I am
seldom idle.

Seasonal Therapy

If you don't find me in the kitchen stirring up a batch of cookies or a meal, I will be doing something else to keep me busy. Like the woman in Proverbs 31, I am seldom idle. There are many books and devotions on Proverbs 31 with varying views and perceptions of what the meaning of the verses are for our current culture's women. I have studied them in detail with scrutiny to see if it's realistic to attain these attributes. My takeaway is that the Proverbs 31 woman is active and not idle, has wisdom and understanding, and works with her hands to be a great example for other women. Idleness is what jumps out for me as I can relate to the need to keep active. That is why I like this verse the most:

> She watches over the affairs of her household and does not eat the bread of idleness.
>
> PROVERBS 31:27 NIV

I love to share stories about life, and in this section there are several shorter stories related to activities that have kept me from idleness. These are more seasonal as I will stop for a few months and start them later within the year, referring to them as 'therapy.' As I explained in the Food

Therapy chapter, these activities help distract the constant swirling in my mind and keep me busy while working at completing a project. The first one is about gardening.

"It's way too big for your first garden," stated my mother-in-law as I showed her the stakes of each row we plotted out in the ground where our garden would be in the backyard of our rented house. I adamantly replied, "No, it's going to be fine. We want to try many different things and we need this much room."

Fast forward close to forty years after I heard this from my mother-in-law, I was standing looking at our son and daughter-in-law's first garden. When I looked at the huge section of tilled ground ready to be staked out and planted, these very same words rolled off my tongue, "It's way too big for your first garden." At that second, I remembered my mother-in-law's words and wisdom about our first garden, and she was correct. It was a great garden and it was extremely productive, so much so that I did not want to confess to her that she was right; it was way too big for a first attempt. We did not realize the planting part is the easiest—it's the weeding, tilling, and harvesting where the real work comes into play. Gardening is hard work and not for the weak at heart.

My husband and I have been gardening since that first garden. Because we lived out in the country, there has been plenty of space to have huge gardens for many years and we have learned through many trials and errors. We love gardening because it keeps us active in attending to it each day from planting the seeds to the bountiful harvest. It's a lifestyle that we have enjoyed each spring, summer, and early fall that provides great exercise, responsibility, and holistic foods for our family.

Every spring brings a clean slate for a new garden and the determination to learn more about what will produce well and how to grow enough to feed our family. As the size of our family has changed, gardening continues to be something we do because we can bless others with the harvest and still have enough to preserve to last through the winter.

Our preference is to blanch and freeze the majority of the vegetables, while canning only a few things. With both of these preserving methods, I have taught myself or had other women show me how to do it. It's so easy to find 'how to's' online, but the hands-on learning and fellowship I've received through times like this have been memory keepers. It's fun to get together to work and have good conversation and tons of laughs. It's good therapy.

Another activity that is done once or twice a year is making lefse in the late fall before Thanksgiving and Christmas. What's lefse? It's a regional Scandinavian delicacy and a way to use up potatoes. The history about lefse is fascinating, so if you'd like to know where things came from, go search it out. My story about lefse is a fun one because I think it's a God story in how He will answer our smallest request for things our heart desires and bless others in the process.

As a young girl we could receive a few pieces of lefse during the Christmas season and savor each bite of the melt-in-your-mouth treat. I only learned how to make it in my thirties after a friend's mother taught me the step-by-step process. After leaving her house, I was so excited to have learned an old technique from my heritage and I wanted to keep passing it on to the next generation, BUT I did not have any of the special equipment that was needed. I decided that day to start praying for the money to buy the items or somehow find them at an auction or garage sale.

After many months of sending my requests to God for a lefse griddle and all the equipment, He answered my prayer early on a Saturday morning. I had sat down to enjoy breakfast and read the newspaper. Glancing through the classified ads, one popped out at me—For Sale, Lefse Griddle and All Equipment. I called as fast as I could. The selling party said someone had already called but whoever arrived at their house first with cash, it would be theirs. I was out the door with cash in hand to race to the address. I was the first one there and my dream had come true; it was sold to me.

Interestingly, the sellers were a couple in their sixties who were selling the husband's mother's lefse equipment because she had moved into assisted living and they nor the children would be using the items and wanted to make sure it went to a good home and would be used. Sharing my prayer request story with them moved them to tears as they knew it would find our home a good place to rest. The only request they asked was if I would bring a piece of lefse to them so their mother could know her well-used equipment was going to be used for many more years. I agreed.

One week after purchasing the long-awaited equipment, I made my first batch of lefse by myself following the step-by-step instructions exactly how I was shown. They turned out wonderful and I was so excited. While cleaning, I noticed a sticky address label wrapped around the electrical cord. As I read the name, it sounded very familiar from the small community where my brother-in-law and sister-in-law farmed. I called my sister-in-law to inquire about the name and she said, "That's who we rent land from." What a small world or better said, "What a God-coincidence world." As I delivered the lefse, as promised, I shared this last portion of the story to the couple. They were so excited to know of the connection and knew the equipment would be well taken care of and treasured.

It's been several years since I bought the equipment and I have made many, many rounds of lefse with family and friends. It is a time to enjoy each other's company, to laugh, and joke about who can roll the thinnest rounds and who is the best flipper. There is also lots of talk about the main ingredient of potatoes and if instant or real ones make for a moister piece of lefse. There is a continual debate amongst lefse makers whether to use real or instant potatoes. I have made lefse with both types of potatoes and can tell you that when using real potatoes you will get a moister round than instant potatoes. The noticeable difference seems to be when freezing the lefse rounds made with real potatoes you will get a better end product as they keep their moisture better. Compare it for yourself to see which one you prefer; mine in the last several years has been instant. **Check out the recipe I use in Recipes from Sue on page 211.**

One thing is for sure, making lefse is an all-day project and a huge flour mess in the kitchen that is started early in the morning with hopes to have it finished by supper. Even though it is an all-day-long project, I want to keep doing it so the heritage stays alive and I can share the fun God story of how He answers us even in the smallest ways.

During the time that lefse making is happening, I begin my winter hobby of quilting. It helps me stay busy and awake after supper when the couch is calling my name and wanting me to lob out for the rest of the evening, flip through my phone, and accomplish nothing. Quilting came about because I wanted to keep a family tradition going, as both of my grandmothers and a great grandmother quilted. I was the recipient of many of their beautiful quilts and admired their sewing skills. I love being able to display and use these quilts, so I decided to learn how to continue this tradition.

Since my mother did not quilt, it was a perplexing issue to learn how to do this even though I knew how to sew. Quilting is a whole different talent I knew nothing about. The best resource back when I started was going to the library to check out books to begin learning. One of the most beneficial books with detailed help was *Quilting for Dummies.* I needed the step-by-step instructions that were easy to understand. Even though the book suggested NOT to do a t-shirt quilt for your first project, I decided I knew best and tackled it. The gigantic stack of old t-shirts was constantly being moved around and I simply needed them to be gone. So I jumped in and tackled a queen size t-shirt quilt, made of t-shirts, denim jeans, and flannel material.

Yep, baptism by fire! I would highly recommend NOT doing this for your first project because I learned the hard way that it was too difficult for a beginner.

Every year when quilting season starts, it is a creative outlet that allows my artistic side to flourish as I enjoy building my own patterns. I seek out the general idea online which initiates the beginning of the pattern, then I search through the stacks of material I have collected over the years to find what will work the best for the project. It is a satisfying hobby that keeps my hands and mind busy during the long, dark winter evenings. Each year I sew several quilts for others, and while I do, each person is prayed for and thought of as I complete the project.

I've lost track of the number of quilts I've made, as I also have with the number of lefse rounds, and the number of jars of preserved goods, and the years that gardening has been a part of my life. What I know is that each one of these hobbies has touched other people's lives in some way while it has kept idleness at bay and my mind full of gratefulness. Thank you, God, for allowing me to learn and work at these creative outlets.

Trust
God will
provide.

Having Enough Money

Trust and God will provide. That is a great rah rah statement, but how does it actually work when it comes to finances? In my life the answers have come in learning sessions with God. These money lessons have had lasting impressions that have helped us stay on track and share with our sons and others how we must trust God to provide, no matter what the circumstances.

The first lesson was one about saving and giving money. When I landed my first job out of college and was making a nice income, I began to spend the money as fast as I would get it. My future husband watched as money ran through my fingers like water. His parents taught him to save money more than spend it. With this ingrained in him, he couldn't resist putting out a challenge to me as he thought I couldn't even save twenty dollars a week and put it into a savings account. Taking the challenge, I was bound and determined to win. I first had to figure out how to get a savings account because I had never had one.

I did succeed at this test and it was the beginning of a lifestyle of saving more, spending less, and giving too. In my twenties the saving of the majority of my paychecks and living on little was the plan as I had my eyes on many tangible items to purchase. Whatever the cost of the item, I would save up the entire amount needed and then make the purchase. As jobs advanced, I would have the financial institution transfer various amounts into several separate savings accounts once my paycheck was deposited: Christmas gifts, vacation, slush, large purchases. The amount that was left to spend was little so this was the beginning of a thrifty, or should I say cheap, lifestyle.

Cheap, thrifty, frugal, economical, tight, penny pincher, whatever word you want to use to describe saving money, reusing and buying gently used items, and wisely purchasing groceries, I am good at it. And we have never gone without. I am comfortable with the way our lifestyle is and content in the material world. My husband and I will save and reuse more items that others throw away as junk. We find charm in recreating purposeful use out of a thing that was intended for garbage. Nice description to say we're junk collectors! Oh well, it's a fun challenge to see if we can bring life back to something and use it for several more years. It allows us to stay active and use our brains to get things to work again.

Saving for the future, may it be six months from now or ten to twenty years, is a wise decision for having money set aside for the emergency needs like when an appliance breaks or a vehicle dies. Having funds for the unexpected needs that arise brings you a safety net which allows for peace to remain in your finances. How about long-term uncertainties like losing a job, or an accident that can change the entire dynamics of your existence? If you have been consistent in being good with your money, paying your bills on time, saving, and giving, you can trust God to take care of you and your family.

> *Teach those who are rich in this world not to be proud and not to trust in their money, which is so unreliable. Their trust should be in God, who richly gives us all we need for our enjoyment. Tell them to use their money to do good. They should be rich in good works and generous to those in need, always being ready to share with others. By doing this they will be storing up their treasure as a good foundation for the future so that they may experience true life.*
>
> 1 TIMOTHY 6: 17-19 NLT

Letting God teach me in the area of finances has been the answer to the most difficult equation. He has been the best Teacher as I have been directed by His Word about tithing and giving. Tithing can be a subject with varying opinions within individuals, even within your own household. That is why it is so important to search and study God's Word for yourself so the best decision can be made for your individual situation. The guideline I have followed is to tithe where I am taught and fed spiritually, and generously give to those in need when I am prompted. The rule of thumb I have followed is when your paycheck arrives, use the following method:

10/10/10 Method

Tithe Ten Percent
Save Ten Percent
Give Ten Percent

I have done the best I can at following this guideline, but I have huge room for improvement. When I work at the 10/10/10 method, it works. When I don't, God still blesses me and that continues to show me I MUST keep working at His command so He continues to show up in my life. He proves it to me time and time again with countless material and spiritual growths through all my years of walking with Him. Thank you, Papa God, for taking care of me as I continue to work on weaknesses.

Be sure to set aside a tenth of all your fields produce each year.

DEUTERONOMY 14:22 NIV

Each of you must bring a gift in proportion to the way the Lord your God has blessed you.

DEUTERONOMY 16:17 NIV

The next lesson was how God will provide and take care of us no matter how much money we have. When God pulled me away from my corporate job to stay home with our young sons, the loss of the money I was contributing to the family was going to make a significant difference in how we paid our expenses. The financial adjustment to our growing family was a strain to our pocketbook. Even with a few sideline businesses, I was only able to cover a minimal portion of the expenses compared to before. Each payday we had enough to pay the essential bills, put money in savings, and buy groceries. However, the grocery money was cut by more than half of what I was used to having. Using coupons and becoming extremely creative with limited pantry items was high priority if we were to survive this financial adjustment. No more were the times of shopping freely to buy items without hesitation. Now it had to be a strategic planning session prior to entering the store.

Each week I would methodically prepare the grocery list by pricing out each item from grocery ads and totaling the amount to make sure I had enough money to cover what was on the list. The list needed to be followed like a well-tracked map down each store aisle. The boys would help find each item and put only the specific quantity in the cart to make sure we did not exceed the budgeted amount. Week after week I would become frustrated about the chore that previously was one of simply strolling the aisle and putting anything I wanted in the basket, not giving a whim of thought to what the price of the item was. It was a labor intensive, mentally exhausting process to stay within the guidelines of what we could spend each week.

During one of the times I was preparing the list, God nudged me to stop the bad attitude about not having enough. We had plenty. We were not starving, and He was providing for us every week. This is when the following scripture was emphasized to me—in short I call it the bird of the air verse. It is the reminder from God's view of how much He will care for us compared to the birds of the air.

*Look at the birds of the air; they do not sow or reap or
store away in barns, and yet your heavenly Father feeds
them. Are you not much more valuable than they?*

MATTHEW 6:26 NIV

I began to repeat this verse over in my head to remind myself who was taking care of us and that my attitude needed
to change to one of gratitude for all God was doing for us.
I prayed for my sour attitude to be turned positive. God
put the cherry on top of this lesson when I decided the
next week to turn my bitter attitude into a challenge of
sorts to stop the negativity. Changing the somber task to
one of a game to see how close I could come within cents
to the dollar of the allocated money I had to buy groceries.
This idea began slowly but ramped up the positive mindset
week after week, until I was excited to go each time to see
if I could get within pennies of the budgeted amount.

And then it happened, the week when the grocery bill
final total compared to my well-prepared and followed list
came within cents of the budget! Woohoo, I had achieved
the goal! Making the budget and having a positive attitude
while accomplishing it. My excitement was too much to
celebrate by myself so I called my husband to announce my
win. God had turned my negative thoughts to positive ones
in the simple tasks of every day life.

Another lesson was to help teach our sons how waiting for big purchases is a good idea. With our two sons
being five years apart, the older one has been the spokes-
person for them on several occasions when there was a
major thing they wanted to explain to my husband and

me. When they were approximately ten and five years old, it was announced that they had saved enough money between them to purchase two Nerf guns that were around thirty dollars each. They were ready to go to the store and buy them and wanted me to drive them there. Thirty dollars for one toy gun—wow, that sure seemed expensive.

They had counted out their money, grabbed their coats, and were in the van fast as could be once I said, "Sure we can go *look* to see if the store has them." In their minds they heard, "Sure, we can go and buy them." Once we got to the toy aisle, they had to look over all of the options even though they were set on a specific model. As I looked over all those available, they sure seemed to be expensive and I questioned if they would really like the one they were ready to choose.

My husband and I have been price shoppers because we have had financial goals to meet and every penny we earned needed to be allocated in a wise way. This especially came true once I left my corporate job and became a stay-home mom. There was little to no room for extras and that was communicated often to the boys.

Even though the boys had enough money and could have made the purchase that day, I said, "Let's do some price shopping at another store and if you still want them tomorrow, we will come back and buy them. It's wise to sleep on it when you're making a big purchase. You may change your mind by tomorrow and decide not to buy it or buy something else." Reluctantly the boys walked out of the store empty-handed and not throwing a fit.

Unfortunately, the next store did not have the same model of the toy gun so no comparison could be done. They wanted to immediately go back to the store where we first started to buy their big purchase. But I stuck to my guns (pun intended) and we went home to have them sleep on it. The rest of the day they moped around as they felt deprived of their goal of spending their money.

The next morning could not have arrived fast enough for them as they woke up early, ready to go back to the store to buy their toy guns. They were afraid they wouldn't be there and the faster we got there the better. But I needed to make sure I followed through with my point on this whole issue, saying, "Did you really think this through? Are you sure you want to spend thirty dollars on one toy gun when you could buy several other items?" A loud succinctly said, "YES" along with, "Mommm, let's just go."

To my disappointment that day, we added two toy guns with Styrofoam bullets to the collection of their toys. I questioned if my lesson on financial waiting proved anything. This story is the one they recall when I mention to them as grown sons the need to wait before they buy. I've asked them as adults, "What did you learn from the lesson?" Their response; "You are cheap and we could hardly wait until the next day."

Not all our parenting lessons work as we think they will, but if it leaves a memorable impression in their minds in addition to a fun memory for grown children, it is worth it.

The waiting game for big purchases is a successful tool along with other steps you can take to achieve financial freedom.

Steps to Financial Freedom

Money to Savings

With every paycheck, automatically put money into savings. Creating several savings accounts for specific things additionally is beneficial. Example: Christmas Present Savings, Insurance Savings (auto, house, renters, etc.), Property Tax Savings (if not included in mortgage payment), Household Savings (big purchases like furniture, appliances, remodeling, replacement for breakdowns), Trip Savings (annual trips).

Credit Cards

Only have a maximum of one or two credit cards. Limit store credit cards and only sign up to get one if it's for a major purchase discount. Once it is paid off, stop using it and call the company to delete the account. The biggest must is paying off credit card balances every month.

Bill-Paying System

Create a system of knowing when the bills are due and what paycheck will be paying for those bills. This helps to see if there may be less to buy other necessities in one paycheck. Set up bill balance monthly payments for utilities so every month is the same amount regardless of your usage.

List of Needed Items

Continually keep a running list of items the household needs, like groceries, toiletries, paper goods, outside items, etc. This allows for wise planning and not running completely out of the item.

Entertainment and Dining Out

Limiting eating out to once a week for dinner time for the family, and allocating it as your entertainment, will accomplish two things. How? It's entertaining to watch how your children behave while you're eating out! Okay, the young moms don't find this funny, but as a mom who has been in your shoes, it is good practice for our young children to learn how to behave properly in public and show good manners and patience. If all works well and the dining out was successful, a fun adventure will be the reward. Our rewards did not have a monetary fee tagged to them; they were drives in the country, dirt biking rides, or playing at a fun outdoor playground. Other times we would splurge and do more elaborate adventures like going to a water park, or ski trip on the train.

Children Expenses

A reasonable guideline to set during child-rearing years is that each child can be in one to two sport activities and one music activity outside of school until junior high. At this time they traditionally make their final selection of what activities they will focus on. This idea helped us know the approximate costs on an ongoing basis for fees, equipment, travel expenses, lessons, etc.

Being good stewards of our financial resources has been a challenge and at times has led to arguments. Yet, when we have stayed open-minded to discuss the situation and lean on God's guidance, good results have happened. Benefits like paying off a home mortgage before retirement, being able to purchase without borrowing, having money to purchase emergency items, and knowing the funds needed for retirement years will be available. I believe God will give us what we need, when we need it.

Be sensible and store up precious treasures—don't waste them like a fool.

PROVERBS 21:20 CEV

God can bless you with everything you need, and you will always have more than enough to do all kinds of good things for others.

2 CORINTHIANS 9:8 CEV

It was
more than
the walls
within a
building that
held godly
functions.

Go to Church

During the first few years after alcohol and drug treatment and being active in a twelve-step program, I slowly accepted the possibility there may be a God. I didn't know what I believed in and decided to take the cotton out of my stubborn ears to hear what others said about God. This is when willingness began to take hold to possibly consider that this godly image I'd seen in pictures with a white flowing rob, long hair, and beard could help me. With only a teaspoon full of willingness, I was now able to listen to others share how this God in their lives was seemingly like a real person. It seemed bizarre to me and on the scale of being way out there in craziness, but I kept on listening. I'd ask questions and they would get answered with no books or scripture being pushed my way. This non-threatening behavior opened a curiosity in me to explore the possibility that I too may be able to have this type of God in my life.

I really didn't know if this God would welcome me or forgive me for all the dark years of my past, but I accepted an invitation to attend a mainstream, traditional church. I began attending regularly and I liked the pastor and the sermons with thought-provoking messages. I liked singing and was invited to join the choir. All of it reminded

me of the church of my childhood that we would sporadi-
cally attend. Attending each Sunday was considered being
in good standing while missing a Sunday seemed to put
shame on my shoulders. With limited depth in any Bible
teaching and my willingness teetering on unbelief, I would
mostly shy away and eventually not attend.

While continuing to attend twelve-step meetings and
feeling a spiritual connection there, I began to use the group
as a Higher Power. This concept was short-lived as the feeling quickly faded once I left the rooms. The one thing they
kept on saying was, "You can form your own concept of
God and have a personal relationship with Him." Well,
what did that mean? I went to the traditional church building and the presence of God seemed to be there but was
gone when I left, which was the same as the twelve-step
meeting. This personal relationship and my own concept
of God was puzzling and constantly on my mind. During
an overnight business trip, I was in my hotel room reading
when my continual perplexing thoughts of God came to
me again. This was the second time in my recovery life
that I sensed a presence of peace that emotionally overtook
me. Tears began streaming down my face and this notion
of a personal God whom I could understand came alive.

Soon after this hotel room encounter, I was invited to
listen to some great music at a church as it was described
as a concert-like setting. Well, if it was going to be anything
like a music concert, I was willing to go.

The church sure didn't look like the churches I'd been
familiar with in the past. It was in a building that was

previously a retail store. There was no steeple or pews, no choir or pastor in a robe. It looked more like a concert venue with rows of chairs in front of a stage that was decked out with all the musical instruments I was accustomed to seeing at music concerts. People were visiting and shuffling around greeting each other and extending warm, outreached hands to welcome me. The atmosphere was mesmerizing and intriguing as my thoughts were, "There's no way this is a church; it must be some type of cult." The music started and it was just like my friend had explained it, like a concert, and I loved it. It was called Christian worship music, which I had never heard of, yet I loved it because it was like rock and roll music with slower songs that were very contemporary.

This invitation was the beginning of many years attending this church; well, actually they called it a fellowship. Anyway, the music is what attracted me to come to a place where God was and it was communicated through His Word, the Bible. In short, it led me to some of the most remarkable and significant foundational years of my new, personal walk with God. A God of my understanding. God was real. He was alive in me as I could feel a change in me.

During these years, I established countless core tools such as studying the Bible; learning how to pray for others, my family, and myself; how to love and tolerate others; understanding the purpose of fasting, worship, and thanksgiving to God; why tithing and giving were needed; and why it was important to parent and raise your children up in the Word of God. I would faithfully attend church every week and participate in as many activities, events, and studies as they would offer. The boys loved the children's church and began to learn so much about God. Going to church became a major priority in my life, as each time we went God met us there.

The messed up person that I was in a non-traditional environment where God met me and didn't care about what my outsides looked like, what job I had, or what my past contained; He was only interested in my inside and the condition of my heart. I was ready to live a new and different life. I wanted to be completely changed from the inside out.

> *It doesn't make any difference now whether we have been circumcised or not; what counts is whether we really have been changed into new and different people.*
>
> GALATIANS 6:15 TLB

> *When someone becomes a Christian, he becomes a brand new person inside. He is not the same anymore. A new life has begun!*
>
> 2 CORINTHIANS 5:17 TLB

I was learning about this tickling feeling inside me that gave me fresh energy and excitement to go on—it was the Holy Spirit. It was like I was a brand new person. I was not going to be the same any more. The past was gone and I was starting a new life.

But when the Holy Spirit comes upon you, you will be filled with power, and you will be witnesses for me in Jerusalem, in all of Judea and Samaria, and to the ends of the earth.

ACTS 1:8 GNT

The fire-like feeling inside of me wanted all of what I could receive. And I was ready to get filled up. I was a fresh canvas ready to be primed and painted to a new masterpiece. The end work would be amazing. For over ten years the learning, seeking, and absorbing was a lifestyle of a new way with God. Eventually my husband joined me and the boys on this journey and together we ventured to learn about and seek God to let Him fix the broken parts in us. We went to Christian music concerts, traveled to listen to evangelists, speakers, and teachers. We witnessed the move of the Holy Spirit and heard prophesies as we continued to allow God to work out in us what only He could.

During this time, we began to understand the structure of churches, denominations, and how man operates in these institutions. As we grew in knowledge and strength, others were witnessing the changes and wanted us to be more involved. We accepted leadership roles and began to witness the many amazing people God has called to do his work, how God actively moves in miracles, and how our fleshly ways also work in the walls of churches. And as a wise, godly woman says often, "We are all just a bunch of people." We began to witness the humanness seeping out and how at times God becomes small and the focus on Him can diminish.

Jesus Christ never changes! He is the same yesterday, today, and forever.

HEBREWS 13:8 CEV

My ideals of what church was supposed to be like were being changed, the four-wall buildings were not all they were cracked up to be. It was more than the walls within a building that held godly functions. The narrow-focused definition I had in my mind was changing. God was moving me to get beyond the conceptions I had formed about church. During this time, I researched the Bible to understand more about what 'church' means. The definition of church in the Greek dictionary was clearly a group of people gathered together. In the New Testament a church is never referred to as a building or a meeting place; it is a fellowship of saints or people of God, a bride of Jesus Christ, saved and sanctified by Him for a union with Himself. All believers in universal fellowship. It's an interesting study and I highly suggest you dig into the subject if you've ever questioned it.

After this study, I moved into a period of time of balancing all the head knowledge about the subject with what my heart seemed to be feeling. The mind is powerful and it yearns to be logically correct, while the heart aches to explode in the pure understanding of living every day free of confusion. The heart was winning and my mind was weakening as God was pulling me closer to a romance with Him. The four-wall building idea slipped out of my mind when the beautiful dance with God came and I allowed Him to overtake me and I would surrender to a new level.

Meeting God each and every day on my level was then, and is now, my main objective.

The question of whether to attend a four-wall church building or not is one that each of us needs to answer privately with God. Each of us will have our own opinion and ideas from our life experiences and studying God's Word. Only you and God know what's best for you. I do know that a close, intimate, personal relationship with God is the best way to get the answer. Be strong enough to know what you believe and determined to understand that others will judge you, but only you have to stand before God and be accountable for your choices.

I give glory and honor back to God for the work He has done in my life.

Twenty-Five

Worship

Sitting at a table with several women at a gun safety event, I was visiting and trying to listen as we got to know each other. It was a weekend event so we'd be spending a lot of time together. During one of the breaks, I heard a woman at the next table say that she was an author. This got my attention as I had begun to write my story and wanted to know more about writing. I kept my eyes open for any opportunity to engage in a conversation with her since she was not in the same group I was in. When lunch time approached, I made my way over to the area where she was sitting to hopefully strike up a conversation. After asking her several questions, I found out that she was a Christian fiction author and was currently working on her most recent book. We agreed to connect with each other and get together for coffee to explore how we could learn from each other. The coffee date was the beginning of a relationship that progressed into us forming a local Christian writers' group. We met weekly for close to a year before she and several others involved had life changes and were no longer available to participate. During the writers' group, we all gained so many wonderful things from each other: encouragement, hope, love for words, and faith that God would bring to life what He wanted in our personal stories through writing.

This woman passed down to me a statement that was shared with her and it is something that will stay with me forever. "Worship God through writing." It was an eye-opening declaration at the time and continues to be one I firmly stand on when weariness sets in as I write. I had not thought of writing as an act of worship. It intrigued me so much that I needed to ponder the meaning.

Worship as defined by Webster's dictionary is to honor or show reverence for, to regard with great respect, honor, or devotion. In other words, in regard to writing, "My writing skill is one from God and by using this talent, the words I believe He is asking me to write, He is communicating to me so others can benefit. By continuing to write, I am obedient to His calling on me, so this is worship unto Him."

When worship is looked at in a more traditional sense, it is when I give glory and honor back to God for the work He has done in my life. For me, worship is communicating and expressing myself through a variety of forms: prayer, singing, dancing, and raising my hands to Him.

Music helps my thoughts and emotions to connect to God. In the Old Testament, David is known for bringing music into the temple services. It communicated in words and instruments the feelings inside David. It does the same for me. It can bring calmness or excitement depending on the rhythm and the words. It promotes freedom in expression and helps me empty my busy thoughts to clear the way for God to bring refreshment to me, may it be from weariness or elation. I can then be reminded of God's greatness, be renewed in the blessings He continues to provide, and be ready to continue on this journey.

You are my God. I worship you. In my heart, I long for you, as I would long for a stream in a scorching desert. I have seen your power and your glory in the place of worship. Your love means more than life to me, and I praise you. As long as I live, I will pray to you. I will sing joyful praises and be filled with excitement like a guest at a banquet.

PSALM 63:1-5 CEV

Believe me, woman, the time is coming when you Samaritans will worship the Father neither here at this mountain nor there in Jerusalem. You worship guessing in the dark; we Jews worship in the clear light of day. God's way of salvation is made available through the Jews. But the time is coming—it has, in fact, come—when what you're called will not matter and where you go to worship will not matter. It's who you are and the way you live that count before God. Your worship must engage your spirit in the pursuit of truth. That's the kind of people the Father is out looking for: those who are simply and honestly themselves before him in their worship. God is sheer being itself—Spirit. Those who worship him must do it out of their very being, their spirits, their true selves, in adoration.

JOHN 4: 21-24 MSG

The simple
moments
are the most
important
ones.

Love My Own Parents

After I wrote my memoir, readers began to ask the question, "How is your current relationship with your parents?" My response, "It's good." Well, good is a quick response to a complicated answer which actually can be extremely lengthy.

Sharing several childhood memories in my memoir explained my view of how I grew up. My life with my parents got messy when I became a self-focused teenager and everything was all about me. My parents dealt with me the best they knew how. It was like a tug of war with each side getting dragged into the mud occasionally. The hell I put my parents through, mostly Mom because she was the main parental figure, was revealed to me as I processed the childhood events in the writings of my story, along with having my own children. As a parent, I would have been hard pressed to know what to do with a child like me. I was definitely on the scale of "extremely difficult to deal with." The incidents I created and the consequences I endured were challenging enough for me, let alone how my parents felt about me and what it did to them personally. It simply was not good. So from my perspective I had many faults from the wreckage of my past which I have worked on and God has cleaned up. I do not blame my parents for how I turned out. I am at peace with my past and with my relationship with them. So back to the original question, "How is your current relationship with your parents? Good."

To explain a little further, God was working at breaking down walls of unhealthy behaviors in me. I justified many reasons to stay bitter at my parents for a long time, but when God's love and compassion was given to me so freely, I could not maintain the hardness. God's wisdom was shining on me and maturity in my life journey was needed. He would not allow me to hold deep grudges nor hang on to personal desires that my parents change to people I wanted them to become. The humbling of my heart and the willingness to love others just as they are was what advanced my relationship with my parents.

I had no more excuses for why I needed to stay angry and bitter. I realized my time with them is too short and it needs to be cherished instead of harbored in hate. Living without regrets and showing respect no matter what was done or said in the past had to be done. God worked on me to release the hostility by having me repeat this scripture over in my head.

Honor your father and mother. Then you will live a long, full life in the land the Lord your God is giving you.

EXODUS 20:12 NLT

It's by God's grace and Him alone that my bitter heart toward my parents has softened to one who can love them as they did me, unconditionally. I did not arrive at this easily, as it got complicated for a period of time because of my need to hold on to the blame game. But, by God's hand being upon me in the cleanup process, He did the healing and helped me release anger, fear, abandonment issues, and self-justification. God has left me with a caring, loving heart that wants to help them as much as I can.

I believe God has made me new in many ways, and sincerely loving my parents has been a change that I know He did, not me. The magnifying glass of judgment that was extremely critical of their parenting skills got turned on me once I became a parent. It's not easy when God doesn't provide an instruction manual with the troubleshooting section highlighted with your own children. He also doesn't lay out the details of how the remainder of our relationship will play out. As my mom has said too many times, "I prayed that you would get a child just like you were." Well, God heard those prayers and most likely sat and laughed when I struggled with knowing what to do with our sons.

Parenting is not for the faint at heart. It changes your entire life and how you view the world. When trouble gets thrown into the picture, it seems like it's the end, yet I have decided it needs to be viewed as a fork in the road. It may not be the one I would choose to go down, yet when I make the decision to hold God's hand and let him guide me, it tends to be easier. The biggest challenge is continuing to hold His hand.

As the years pass, we all change. Accepting each other for who we are and trying not to make each other into something that we may never be is vital. It takes less energy to accept than to harbor hard feelings. God seems to honor this when my heart has been softened and I see others in a different light. There has been no need to bring the past up in my mind or to them. So each day with every encounter I pray for goodness and blessings on them.

I never imagined how we would get along in their later years of life. As aging creeps up, it is a somber moment as the transition from child to assisting with caring for your parents happens; it's weird. They call it role reversal and most of us think it will never happen, yet it does. It's a place no one dreams of and if others had told me about it, I couldn't have imagined it. Now, as age takes hold of their bodies and loss of memory creeps in, it's challenging to reflect back on what was, so it's essential to focus on what is. Today is what it is, and today is what needs to be enjoyed. The simple moments are the most important ones.

As a new reality sets in, I realize it's the beginning of a grieving process. Change is inevitable and it must be embraced to accept what's happening as a normal course on the journey of life. Staying positive and happy to enjoy the simple moments is a key to a great ending.

Love-in-Laws

"No, not right now." "I'm not ready, I need more time."

My schooling and career path have been in the field of business. I could not understand the girls who wanted to be nurses or doctors when we were asked in school, "What do you want to be when you grow up?" Not once did it cross my mind to be a nurse, even though my mom was a Registered Nurse by trade. The blood, oozing wounds, foul smells, and the cleaning of body parts which are not intended for viewing by others were all the reasons why I never wanted to be in the medical profession. No sir, it was never going to be my forte. Plus, when God handed out bucket loads of caring, love, and compassion to some people, I only received a cupful.

This lack of love and compassion for others was a lesson God used to work in this area of weakness by placing me in the position to help care for my in-laws, an adventure I was not ready for.

My mother-in-law become quite sick and needed one-on-one daily care. All the siblings gathered to discuss options, with one being opening our home to have her and my father-in-law live with us for a period of time. My husband asked me, "Are you okay with the idea? Are you ready for it?" I wanted to answer, "No, not right now. I'm not ready, I need more time." I quickly prayed and took my thoughts and worries of imagining the many "what ifs" captive and tried to hear God in the situation. There was no loud sounding answer, yet a continual phrase in my head saying, "We can't say no." With this quick evaluation, our answer was yes. I loved her too much to say no. My mother-in-law loved me like her own daughters; how could I say no?

The next step was getting them moved into our home. Converting an office to a bedroom with a new coat of paint and shuffling furniture to make it their new room. The remainder of the house had to be viewed by professional eyes who knew the needs of elderly with walking assistance apparatuses. Removing throw rugs, adding a stabilizing bar next to the toilet, and adding a chair to the bathroom were a few of the changes that were made. We were determined to make this the best, unpleasant situation for all of us.

The next thing I knew, the details of her daily needs were given to me while I was standing by her hospital bed being instructed by nurses on how to care for an open wound on her leg which needed to be cleaned and dressed three times a day. The instructions were extremely thorough and lengthy. I had the fleeting thought, "No way! I want nothing to do with this oozing, messy wound." However, there was no other option because our YES was YES. As I intently watched the step-by-step training on the wound care, my mother-in-law looked at me with eyes of appreciation and I knew she would do the same for me.

The daily needs and care of elderly parents are something a person doesn't think of until the day comes and you are face-to-face with the reality. There were more questions than answers in the everyday movements of life: what foods do they need to stay on a low sodium, high fat diet; what pills need to be taken; when are the doctors' appointments? I had to lean into God, and He would have to provide ALL the answers.

The entire journey of having my in-laws live in our home, and then them moving to an assisted living home, and eventually having my mother-in-law passing away was all in a time span of approximately nine months. All our lives were turned upside down and each person adjusted the best they knew how during a time which none of us had ever experienced.

The lesson God was teaching was ignited in my heart because of love, the love He poured out for me I was pouring out to my in-laws, my love-in-laws. Love will stretch a person farther than they have ever been moved. At the beginning of our new arrangements, things were going great because I was in control of it; the painting of the room, cooking for their dietary needs, organizing medical appointments, and tracking symptoms were all in my wheelhouse of skills that I could handle. But adjusting to the constant care and need to be available at all times was a shock to my independent ways. The rigid schedule was focused on caring for the wound three times a day as it became increasingly difficult to do any other activities outside the house. The reality became clear, the wound came first—anything else needed to be let go of. My life was in a world I had never experienced before besides possibly when the boys were infants and needed constant care.

After a few months of the new routine, I was trying to have some quiet time with God and I just started crying because there was no quiet any more. It had disappeared because the TV volume was extremely high. I could even hear it when I tried to tuck myself in the farthest corner of the basement to seek God. The selfish tears were seeping out of a halfway fixed up woman who needed to lean more on God in the noisy times. The mature portion of the woman in me put on the best happy, smiling face possible to try not to show the insensitivity leaking out. Tears were held back long enough for me to escape to our bedroom where the weeping was released. On one occasion as I sat on the bed staring out the window thinking, "What did I get myself into? I'm never going to be able to do what I want to do," I heard in a loud, nearly audible voice, "It's NOT about YOU! Be of service and love."

The tears flowed only a bit longer before the reality of love struck my heart and I knew deep within myself the selfishness had to stop. From that moment on, my thoughts changed because God was doing a work in me that only He understood. I needed to be a vessel of love, compassion, patience, kindness, gentleness, and grace. He was doing for me what I could not do for myself. It would happen only when I was willing to let go and trust Him.

As the willingness came and I quit resisting my selfish needs, clarity was in view as I was able to see through new glasses of love and patience. I learned to enjoy the simple moments like when we had to wait in a doctor's office that was running several hours behind schedule and my mother-in-law and I belly laughed so loud people in the waiting area turned to look at us because we found humor in her swiping my father-in-law's cap to place on her head, only to have him shake his head in frustration and walk away from us. She was making us have fun in a serious situation, even though she was under the heavy influence of pain medication which she needed to take to endure the weekly appointment of cleaning out a life-threatening wound.

The weekly 200-plus mile round trip to the wound care clinic became a joy because of God's fresh view He gave my eyes. From the beginning of the trip each week, we'd start out with a little song as we buckled up to hit the road. My mother-in-law's positive attitude never weakened as I'd say, "And, we're off." Her response in childlike melody was singing, "We're off to see the wizard, the wonderful wizard of Oz." Each time I'd wait for it and without fail, she'd sing it and I'd get the biggest grin on my face as my father-in-law would be shaking his head with wonder at the two of us and our giddy humor from a simple statement. It became a comforting expectation when we didn't want to go during bad weather with frigid negative zero temperatures. Now, every trip down the same route is a fond memory as I remember each physical location where she would loudly announce it by name. How I'd relive those moments in a second if I could bring her back.

God's schoolroom during this time was filled with lessons; my selfishness was stripped, compassion was gained for the hurting, my patience and tolerance were substantially increased, the fast-paced speed I was accustomed to was slowed, and the biggest lesson—life was NOT about ME, it was about others.

When the end of this journey came on July 28, 2014, my heart knew it would never be the same. The lessons learned are too numerous to name, and truthfully, I will never know all of them until death passes my way. Until then, I know the mark God put on my heart was etched by my mother-in-law's lasting impressions and her pure love for others and for life.

When the day came to say good bye, I shared this tribute to a woman who made a mark in my heart....

Thank you for being a second mother to me. You were loving, caring, a good listener, and non-judgmental.

Our family background and ages were very different, yet our lives blended well as mother-in-law and daughter-in-law. We should have had many opportunities for tension but there was more tenderness and affection expressed for each other. Thank you for loving me like a daughter.

From the first day I met you, until the last day with you, I will cherish each memory. You always listened to me about any issue or problem and would give your two cents about it BUT never made me feel my thoughts were wrong. You mostly listened and supported me no matter what position you took. You showed me how to work hard in the home and yard. You taught me how to cook and would take my call to answer the silliest of questions about cooking. You simply listened and would tell me what you would do. That's what I loved about you.

Through the years you would always help us with the boys and for that I am extremely grateful! You were the best at spoiling them with their favorite treats: candy bags when they left the lake, peanut butter and jelly sandwiches with chocolate covered candies, cinnamon rolls with extra frosting, waffles with maple syrup spilling over each square, the newest soda drink or pop tart was common each week the boys came to the lake—you were the BEST grandma!

Thank you for all the good times and making us feel at home at the lake. I promise to take good care of things there and I will make sure there are always LOTS of flowers, especially geraniums.

Thank you for allowing us to help care for you in the last several months. My Mondays will NEVER be the same—I will always think of you and our long trips to the wound care clinic. Thank you for showing me such a good attitude through such a terrible ordeal. I will never forget the way you would start singing a song as we would be driving off when I would say, "We're off," and you would cheerfully sing, "We're off to see the wizard, the wonderful wizard of Oz!" You made me laugh and for that I'm eternally grateful.

I know you are with our heavenly Father with no more struggles in your lungs, heart, and leg. I will see you there

someday, but until then I miss you every single day!
I Love YOU!

But Ruth said, "Don't force me to leave you; don't make
me go home. Where you go, I go; and where you die, I'll
die, and that's where I'll be buried, so help me God—not
even death itself is going to come between us!"

RUTH 1:16 MSG

My in-laws were a huge factor in me learning to love and show physical affection. They verbally said the words and physically embraced me to show me how to express myself. Their patience with the many events we endured as young parents and the fondness and affection given to our boys is unforgettable. Thank you, God, for letting me have them in my life.

Catch Myself

One year during pumpkin harvest there were nine pumpkins off one plant, and interestingly enough this was a plant that grew out of the compost pile (called a volunteer plant). When it started sprouting, it was working its way amongst four rows of onions. In the past, when volunteer plants began growing, I'd let them do whatever they wanted, just letting them wander and see where they would go and what they would produce. However, in this case, there was a high possibility it may crowd out the onions. The goal was to let both exist together and still get a good harvest from each. To help this cohabitation every few days I would take the long green vines from the pumpkin plant and move them into a narrow path of dirt between rows of onions. When the time extended beyond a few days without redirecting the vines, they would shoot out everywhere, escaping the narrow path I was directing them on. As the pumpkin plant grew bigger, it was harder to keep it in the path. Nearly every day the vine needed to be placed back on the path where I wanted it to go. When it began to mature and find its path, it flourished and continued to go down the set path and only on occasion did it need to be brought back into the predetermined path.

The paths of their ways turn aside, they go nowhere and perish.

JOB 6:18 NKJV

I have felt like this volunteer plant during times in my life, finding it extremely hard to stay on the course to God seemed to be directing me. Our lives can feel like the pumpkin vines moving out of the narrow path that has been set for us by God. Our individual journey is unique for each of us with some paths being extremely narrow and others broader. Fully surrendering and acknowledging God daily, He will help keep us on this narrow path. Once we are on it, it feels right yet still challenging as it brings difficulties, yet we know we must continue on the narrow path He has set before us. God begins to teach us "Good Orderly Direction."

Enter through the narrow gate. For wide is the gate and broad is the road that leads to destruction, and many enter through it. But small is the gate and narrow the road that leads to life, and only a few find it.

MATTHEW 7:13-14 NIV

When we get off track, God with His kindness gently places us back on track so we can continue to grow and mature. During the growing process we have free will that likes to take over. Shoots of temptation, growths, and spurts come out on their own as we want to either seek new ground or old familiar ways. This is when we have a choice to bend our knee to God as He gently moves us back on track or we will continue off course and give way to the temptations that pull us, with sprouts shooting out everywhere.

The interesting part about this analogy is that it's not IF we go off track but WHEN. Just as the squirmy shoots from the vine grow quickly and wander off the narrow path, we must stay in connection with God daily so He can pull us back and set us firmly back on track. This can feel sad and remorseful as we realize what happened, yet God teaches us to come back to Him quickly, confessing our mistakes, saying, "I'm sorry. Please forgive me." Then we get back on the track.

How does this look in every day life? Learning to "catch ourselves" when we are being misdirected in a behavior that we don't want to be in is the key. If we can catch ourselves, we have a split second to choose a different reaction. The biggest step in growing in this "catch" step is when we actually do notice or "catch ourselves"; this is when the progress keeps happening.

Working hard at catching yourself in the action that is being worked on in your life is a tremendous accomplishment in the cycle of changing a behavior. The decision can be made at this very instant, do we stay in it or get out? Can we catch ourselves?

Starting this behavior pattern change takes time, sometimes a long time. Let me emphasize this: sometimes a loooong time! Practice, practice, practice. Just like learning how to catch a ball, it takes practice to become good at knowing what to do when the ball comes flying at you. It's a split-second decision to move out of the way or stay in the path of the ball and get hit. So, the practice to catch yourself and apply healthier words to replay in your thoughts, actions, and behaviors takes many attempts but it's worth every minute. You will feel better about yourself, so your head can be held high knowing God loves you. We are beautifully and wonderfully made by Him.

Here are a few of my fighting back scriptures when this attack comes on me. The first statement is the one I suggest to use immediately when we catch ourselves. The decision needs to be quick to squelch the fast arrows of inadequacies that try to fill our minds when we feel like we did it again and nothing is changing.

Get behind me Satan

Jesus turned and said to Peter, "Get behind me, Satan! You are a stumbling block to me; you do not have in mind the concerns of God, but merely human concerns."

MATTHEW 16:23 NIV

Additionally, there are other verses I've worked on so that they come easily when I'm tempted to go down a negative thought trail of destruction. You can find a full list of other powerful, self-claiming verses to help you believe what God knows of the person He's made you to be. **Refer to Reason to Pray on page 95 and a list of Daily Prayers on page 99.**

I'm the head and not the tail, above, and not beneath

The LORD will make you the head, not the tail. If you pay attention to the commands of the LORD your God

that I give you this day and carefully follow them, you
will always be at the top, never at the bottom.

DEUTERONOMY 28:13 NIV

Jesus is my cornerstone

...built on the foundation of the apostles and prophets,
with Christ Jesus himself as the chief cornerstone.

EPHESIANS 2:20 NIV

I trust you Father God with all my heart

Trust in the LORD with all your heart and lean not on
your own understanding; in all your ways submit to
him, and he will make your paths straight.

PROVERBS 3:5-6 NIV

When I work at living life to the best of my ability which
includes prayer, staying connected with God, and being
willing to keep working on whatever He gives me to do, it's
a success! Catching myself is the whole goal as I progress
in this journey with God. To be willing to have God-con-
sciousness and to be still enough so I can hear His still,
small voice telling me what the next step will be. Then having the courage to take the next step while staying in peace
with what He has told me to do, and then taking the action
to do it.

The phrase "catching myself" is one I hope you can
hang onto because we are imperfect people living this
thing called life out and we will never arrive; we only get
to keep practicing. The best I can do is catch myself when I
sense things are not how God wants them to go, then I can

change course and redirect to a different, hopefully better, behavior or action if I've been spending time with God. This is living life to the best of my ability.

Twenty-Nine

Endurance
Until the End

After walking with God for several years and learning that each day there will be ups and downs, it simply comes to the point where I need to refocus and ask myself, "How do I want to live today?" This question helps me to stay close to the present moment and keeps things in perspective and real. By not focusing on yesterday and certainty NOT tomorrow, it narrows the focus to just today. I may have regrets and want to relive things from my past or push away dreams of the future. Well, it comes down to asking myself the question, to get the focus back to the here and now, my priorities have changed. Today I want to learn how to enjoy the day for whatever it brings; to see nature and its majestic beauty without passing it by, and to continue developing personal relationships with God, my husband, and my boys.

During the last half of my life, after the boys were grown and had left the house, after experiencing my in-laws' passing away, and my parents' health begin to deteriorate, my dreams have once again changed. The dreams have begun to be narrowed to simply being in the here and now, in the little moments within the day like when a hummingbird flutters at the feeder to drink the nectar, or capturing a picture of a butterfly sitting on a flower. These have become the favorite parts of the day. The health in my body and staying spiritually fit with God are my primary focuses.

The dreams of today are not the dreams of yesterday. My dreams will keep changing. The once beloved wish to have this and that all changed to maintaining a daily connection with God, to holding on to love, trust, family, and friends. Some fun bucket list ideas run quickly by my thoughts and I hope they happen, but if they don't I know I will stay satisfied with every dream God allowed to come true.

The key for my life is to stay connected with God, keep it simple, and enjoy the journey. Knowing that God has made me strong through my weaknesses, I can endure anything with Him by my side. May you do the same and be reminded of what the verses in Isaiah say in maintaining hope and enduring until the end is near.

Have you not known? Have you not heard? The Lord is the everlasting God, the Creator of the ends of the earth. He does not faint or grow weary; his understanding is unsearchable. He gives power to the faint, and to him who has no might he increases strength. Even youths shall faint and be weary, and young men shall fall exhausted; but they who wait for the Lord shall renew their strength; they shall mount up with wings like eagles; they shall run and not be weary; they shall walk and not faint.

ISAIAH 40:28-31 ESV

Epilogue

The people I've met on my journey of life make me speech-less. Some I remember for wrong reasons while others will always stay close to my heart. When I was new and on fire for God, a woman who took me under her wing at church to lead and guide me through the newness of my walk will be embedded in my heart and mind until I reach heaven.

Her family was in the military and stationed in our com-munity. When you become friends with a military fam-ily, that's part of their introduction because it identifies them as not growing up from around the area. During our introduction to each other and while we got to know one another, it never dawned on me that they would be leav-ing. After several years of being influenced, enjoying each other's company, and our children playing together, they were informed of their new home and would be leaving our community.

A huge celebration was planned and held at the church we both attended. It was a great time as we listened to peo-ple share how this amazing family impacted so many as they were stationed in our midst. I wanted to close my ears and run to the bathroom to hide my tears as her departure would leave a humongous hole in my heart. I had never gotten so close to someone and enjoyed their company as

I did with her. It was one of the first true, meaningful relationships I experienced in my new life walking with God.

When someone leaves my life because of various circumstances or I leave theirs, I have used the lasting words she said to me and have made them my own. She looked me in the eyes while gently holding my shoulders and said, "This is not good-bye; it's a see you later. We will see each other in heaven." It has been over twenty years since I've seen her, and I hang on to this statement.

As I leave you and continue to walk the path of life, I say so long and the departing statement, "I love you my friend. Keep doing life and see you later."

Recipes from Sue

I pray you enjoy these recipes as much as I have when I've prepared them for those I love. Cooking and baking is an outlet for me to release stress and others enjoy the benefits of it. When recipes are shared, I thank the giver and try to remember them by saying a prayer whenever I use their recipe. As you use these recipes, please remember me and say a prayer for me; it would be a tremendous blessing. I hope you enjoy them as much as I have. May God bless your hands and skills as you make these dishes.

Blueberry Lemon Bread

Love this combination of flavors, a fresh, springtime taste.

¼ c plus 2 Tbsp butter, softened
1 c sugar
2 eggs
1½ c flour
1 tsp baking powder
Pinch of salt
½ c milk
2 tsp lemon juice
1 c blueberries, frozen or fresh
2 tsp flour
⅓ c sugar
3 tsp lemon juice

Cream butter, gradually add 1 c sugar, and beat until well blended. Add eggs, one at a time. Combine flour, baking powder and salt to cream mixture, alternating with milk. Stir in 2 tsp lemon juice. In separate bowl coat blueberries with 2 tsp flour, fold into batter. Pour batter into a well-greased loaf pan. Bake @ 350 degrees for 55 minutes or until toothpick inserted in center comes out clean.

Combine ⅓ c sugar and 3 tsp lemon juice in small saucepan. Heat until sugar dissolves. Poke several holes with a wooden spoon handle into top of loaf; pour lemon juice mixture over warm bread, allowing mixture to soak into bread. Cool bread in pan for 30 minutes.

Dilly Bread

Quick bread, best made to have with soup or chili. It freezes well when wrapped in wax paper and then a plastic bag.

¼ c warm water
1 pkg active dry yeast—dissolve together
Add—1 egg
1 Tbsp butter
1 tsp dill weed
1 tsp salt
1 c cottage cheese, heated
2 Tbsp sugar
¼ tsp soda
1 Tbsp minced onion
2¼ c flour

Mix ingredients together in order listed. Let sit in bowl for 1 hour, stir down, put in greased bread pan, let rise 30-40 minutes. Bake @ 350 for 30-40 minutes.

Double-Quick Dinner Rolls

Made for Thanksgiving and Easter because they are quick yet are great homemade rolls.

Single Batch	*Double Batch*
¾ c warm water	1½ c warm water
1 pkg instant yeast	2 pkg instant yeast
¼ c sugar	½ c sugar
1 tsp salt	2 tsp salt
2¼ c flour	4½ c flour
1 egg	2 eggs
¼ c shortening	½ c shortening

Dissolve yeast in water. Add sugar, salt, and ½ of the flour. Beat thoroughly 2 minutes. Add egg and shortening. Beat in gradually remaining flour. Let rise in bowl 30 minutes in warm place. Stir down batter and drop into greased muffin tin pan. Let rise 30 minutes until doubled.

Bake @ 425 degrees for 10 minutes.

Monkey Bread

A favorite of our younger son who would eat these every morning if he was allowed.

---

3 cans refrigerator biscuits—cut in ¼ pieces and shake into ½ c white sugar and 2 tsp cinnamon

---

Place sugared biscuits in a well-greased bundt pan.

Melt 1 stick butter with 1 c brown sugar. Boil 1 minute. Pour over biscuits.

Bake at 350 degrees for 35 minutes. Cool in pan for 10 minutes. Turn onto a foil lined plate. Do not cut—just pull apart.

Pizza Dough

Best dough that was given to me by my sister-in-law. It makes enough for two crusts, one for savory pizza and one for dessert pizza or freeze one for later.

---

1 pkg instant yeast
1 ¼ c warm water
2 Tbsp oil
1 tsp salt
4 c flour

Dissolve yeast in water. Stir in oil. Mix flour and salt together, stir into oil-water mixture. Knead on surface or mix on knead level on mixer until smooth and elastic. Knead dough by hand for 15 minutes on a flour surface until elastic or by mixer with bread hook, knead for 2-3 minutes on a low level. Shape in ball, place in greased bowl, brush with oil, cover with damp cloth. Let rise until double about 2 hours.

Bake @ 450 degrees 10-15 minutes.

Best Pie Crust Ever

Flaky crust from a friend's mother-in-law which has never failed me. It withstands liquids from meat or fruit pies and does not get soggy.

---

1 c white solid shortening
2½ c flour
2 tsp sugar
½ tsp salt

Mix in mixer on low speed to get to crumbly stage.

In liquid measuring cup strain 2 egg yolks, reserving whites. Add milk to measure ⅔ c.

Add liquid to flour crumbles. Mix on low speed until ball forms.

Roll out pie crust. There is enough for 2 crusts. Paint egg whites on pie shell before adding fruit ingredients. Can also paint egg whites on top crust if desired.

Cherry Coffeecake

A favorite of our older son with a great taste of cherries and a great tasting crust.

½ c butter
¾ c sugar
2 eggs
½ tsp vanilla

Beat all ingredients together. Add following:

1½ c flour
½ tsp salt
¾ tsp baking powder

Place ½ to ⅔ of the batter in a 9x13 greased pan.

Spoon 1 or 2 can(s) cherry pie filling mixed with ¼ tsp almond extract over batter evenly. Spoon the remaining batter over the top of pie filling.

Bake 350 degrees for 25 minutes or until golden brown and toothpick inserted in cake portion comes out clean.

Top with powdered sugar glaze.

Chocolate Chip Cookies

Hands down the best recipe when mixed in this order with butter softened, not melted. Given to me from a good friend whom I think of and pray for each time I make these cookies. These can be made into bars if you don't want to make cookies. They freeze well.

Full Batch	Half Batch
1⅓ c butter	½ c + 3 Tbsp butter
4 eggs	2 eggs
2 c brown sugar	1 c brown sugar
1 c white sugar	½ c white sugar
4 tsp vanilla	2 tsp vanilla

Beat all ingredients together until fluffy. Then add following ingredients:

5 c flour	2 ½ c flour
2 tsp baking soda	1 tsp baking soda
2 tsp salt	1 tsp salt
2 bags (12 oz) chocolate chips	1 bag (12 oz.) chocolate chips

Bake @ 350 degrees for 12 minutes.

Chocolate Frosting

This is the secret recipe for what some have said are the best brownies ever. Top boxed brownies with this frosting and you too will get the same response.

---

1 stick of room temperature butter
$^2/_3$ c cocoa
3 c powder sugar
$^1/_3$ c milk
Dash vanilla

Beat butter until smooth. Add cocoa until pasty looking, then alternate adding powdered sugar and milk until smooth.

Add vanilla, beat until light and fluffy. Spread and refrigerate any leftovers.

Frozen Apple Coffee Cake

Given to me from my mother-in-law and a great way to use an abundance of apples.

½ stick butter, softened
1 tsp baking powder
1 c sugar
1 tsp baking soda
3 eggs
½ tsp salt
1 tsp vanilla
1 c sour cream
2 c flour
2 c chopped apples

Topping:
½ stick butter, softened
1½ c brown sugar
2 tsp cinnamon
1 c chopped walnuts

Cream butter, sugar, eggs and vanilla. Add dry ingredients then sour cream, add apples. Put in two 8-inch greased tin cake pans. For topping, cut butter into brown sugar and cinnamon and nuts. Put on top. Cover with foil and freeze. Bake while frozen, uncovered @ 350 for 50-55 minutes.

Fruit Pizza

Made for so many birthdays and many times every weekend in the summer. It's light and fresh tasting with whatever fresh fruit you like.

Crust:

1 pouch of sugar cookie mix

Mix crust as directed, spread in jelly roll pan and bake at suggested temperature for 8-10 minutes or until golden brown.

Creamy Layer:

1 – 6 oz container of favorite yogurt
(key lime or lemon are a good choice)
1 – 8 oz cool whip
¼ c sugar

Mix together and spread on cooled crust. Layer whatever fruit you desire, good options are kiwi, bananas, mandarin oranges, strawberries, blueberries, raspberries.

Glaze:

¼ c water
¼ c lemon juice
½ c orange juice (if you don't have any use the mandarin orange juice)
¼ c sugar
2 Tbsp cornstarch

Mix all ingredients together, bring to boil, stirring constantly and let cool for at least 10 minutes. Pour glaze over fruit, especially bananas or peaches. This will keep them from turning brown.

Chill for at least one hour.

Neapolitan Cheesecake

A great recipe to make when you like several flavors of cheesecake. This will hit many taste buds and is an all-time favorite.

Crust:

1 c choc wafer crumbs or 12 choc sandwich cookies
3 Tbsp butter

Combine crumbs and melted butter, pat in the bottom of ungreased, 9" spring form pan.

Bake at 350 degrees for 8 minutes, cool.

Layers:

3 – 8 oz pkg cream cheese, softened
¾ c sugar
3 eggs
1½ tsp vanilla

Beat cream cheese and sugar until smooth, no lumps. Beat in 1 egg at a time. This is important so that you get no lumps. Add in vanilla beat again. Divide mixture into 3 portions, about 1⅔ c each.

Dark Chocolate Layer:

2 squares semi-sweet chocolate melted and mixed into
1 portion of cream cheese, pour onto crust.

White Chocolate Layer:
2 squares white chocolate melted and mixed into second portion of cream cheese, pour on top of dark chocolate layer of cream cheese.

Strawberry Layer:
$1/3$ c strawberries, mashed and mixed into third portion of cream cheese, add 6-8 drops of red food coloring, mix well and pour on top of white chocolate layer.

Bake at 425 degrees for 10 minutes, reduce to 300 degrees for 50-55 minutes or until center is nearly set. Remove from oven, immediately run knife around edge. Cool, remove from pan.

Top Drizzle—Dark Chocolate Drizzle:
3 squares semi-sweet chocolate chips
2 Tbsp butter
1 tsp shortening
Melt and drizzle on top of cooled cheesecake.

Top Drizzle—White Chocolate Drizzle:
½ square white chocolate
1 tsp shortening
Melt and drizzle on top of dark chocolate.

Refrigerate for four hours to set.

Granola Bars

I made many batches of these during the boys' swimming years for the go-to recipe when items were needed for bake sale or treats for the team. For an added sweetness, they can be topped with melted chocolate chips.

¼ c butter
½ c honey
1 – 10 oz pkg marshmallows
¾ c chunky peanut butter
½ tsp cinnamon
½ tsp white sugar
5 ½ c Rice Crispies cereal
3 ½ c oatmeal
1 c sunflower seeds
1 c raisins
1 c chocolate chips

Microwave butter, marshmallows, peanut butter and honey until melted, about 2 minutes, 1 minute at a time. Add sugar and cinnamon; stir in. Pour over mixture of cereal, oatmeal, seeds, raisins and chocolate chips; mix well. Spread into a lightly greased 10x15" pan. No baking required! Make sure you coat your hands with butter to aid in spreading the thick mixture.

Old School Apple Crisp

I make this year round with other fruits and is so easy for a last-minute dessert that everyone will WOW about.

---

4 c sliced tart apples (about 4 medium)
½ c packed brown sugar
½ c flour
½ c oats (can use the quick, but rolled is better)
1 tsp cinnamon
⅓ c butter, softened
½ c pecans

Place apple slices in 8x8 baking pan. Mix remaining ingredients thoroughly using a fork, sprinkle over apples.

Bake @ 375 degrees for 30 minutes or until apples are tender and top is golden brown.

Serve warm if possible, and if desired with vanilla ice cream and caramel topping.

Pumpkin Bars

Each fall season this is the first recipe that I make. They are super moist and the frosting is the best.

---

4 eggs
1 c vegetable oil
2 c sugar
2 c pumpkin
2 c flour
2 tsp baking powder
1 tsp baking soda
½ tsp salt
2 tsp cinnamon
½ tsp ginger
½ tsp cloves
½ tsp nutmeg

Mix together eggs, oil, sugar, and pumpkin. Add all the rest of the dry ingredients. Pour into greased and floured jelly roll pan (10x17).

Bake @ 350 degrees for 25-30 minutes. Cool completely. Frost.

Cream Cheese Frosting

1 – 3 oz cream cheese
½ c butter, softened
1 tsp milk
2 c powdered sugar
1 tsp vanilla

Cream together cream cheese and butter. Alternate sugar and milk, then add vanilla.

Balsamic Peppered Chicken

Great winter dish when grilling cannot be done. It was one of my father-in-law's favorite dishes because he liked the juice that can be used to dip each bit of chicken in.

---

4 boneless, skinless chicken breasts
2 tsp lemon pepper seasoning
¼ c chicken broth
2 garlic cloves, minced
1½ tsp olive oil
⅓ c balsamic vinegar
1 Tbsp butter

Sprinkle lemon pepper season on both sides of chicken breasts. Press seasoning into breasts and let sit for 5-10 minutes. In a large frying pan, place oil and heat to medium temp. Add chicken and cook, turning once, about 7 minutes. Remove chicken, keep warm.

In medium bowl, mix together vinegar, broth and garlic; add to frying pan. Cook over medium-high heat, scraping up brown meat bits, about 2 minutes or until mixture is reduced and syrupy. Add butter; stir to melt. Place chicken back in broth mixture to pick up flavors for about 5 minutes.

Smothered Burritos

One of many dishes that is great to make and freeze for a meal to be used later.

---

1 – 1.5 lbs hamburger
1 – 16 oz can refried beans
1 pkt Taco seasoning
Salsa
Cheddar Cheese
8 oz. sour cream
1 can cream of chicken soup
1 can Enchilada sauce
Flour Tortillas

Fry burger with onions if you like. Drain off grease. Mix with taco seasoning. Mix in can of beans and some salsa. Put meat mixture in flour tortillas and place in 9x13 greased pan. In separate bowl, mix soup, sour cream and enchilada sauce. Spread over burritos and top with cheese.

Cover with tin foil and bake @ 350-400 for ½ hour and then take off tin foil and bake for another 15 minutes to get golden brown.

Swedish Meatballs

A favorite recipe on a cold winter day served with mashed potatoes. It makes plenty for great leftovers.

---

4 eggs
1 c milk
8 slices white bread, torn
2 lbs ground beef
4 tsp baking powder
1–2 tsp salt
1 tsp pepper
2 Tbsp shortening
2 cans cream of chicken soup, undiluted
2 cans cream of mushroom soup, undiluted
1 can (12 oz) evaporated milk

In large bowl, beat eggs and milk. Add bread; mix gently and let stand for 5 minutes. Add beef, onion, baking powder, salt and pepper; mix well (mixture will be soft). Shape into 1-inch balls. In a large skillet, brown meatballs in shortening.

Place browned meatballs in an ungreased 9x13 pan. In a bowl, stir soups and evaporated milk together until smooth. Pour over meatballs.

Bake uncovered @ 350 degrees for 1 hour.

French Toast Bake

An all-time favorite of our boys that I'd make on the weekends. Made with leftover heals of bread that many will throw away. Freeze bread in the bag they came in, throw in freezer, and wait until you get around sixteen slices saved.

---

3 eggs
4 Tbsp honey, divided
1½ tsp cinnamon
1 tsp vanilla
1 c milk
15 slices day-old bread (use heals of bread that have been kept in freezer) thaw if frozen
3 Tbsp brown sugar
2 Tbsp butter

In bowl beat eggs with 2 Tbsp honey, vanilla and cinnamon; stir in milk. Dip bread into egg mixture and place in a greased 9x13 pan, arranging by 3 rows of 5 slices of bread, overlapping slices slightly. Cover and chill several hours (8 hrs or overnight if you can). Remove from refrigerator 30 minutes before baking. Sprinkle brown sugar over bread; place small pats of butter over bread along with remaining honey.

Bake @ 350 degrees for 30 minutes.

Lefse

The recipe I began to use after many years of using real potatoes because it is so moist. In a family taste test during Thanksgiving, no one was able to distinguish between a batch made with real or instant potatoes. Recipe is from my daughter-in-law's mother.

---

3 c Hungry Jack instant potatoes
1 Tbsp sugar
1²/₃ tsp salt
1 c powdered milk
3 c boiling water
1 stick butter

Mix the dry ingredients together. In separate container boil the water and melt the butter. Mix them together using a pastry blender or a wooden spoon. Put this mixture in the refrigerator to cool down (overnight or a few hours). When ready to make the lefse, add 1 1/2 cups flour to the potatoes. I use my Kitchen Aid mixer on the lowest speed, add flour and mix until a ball is formed.

Divide into portions, you should get about 16 out of a batch. Roll thin so you can see the red letters on the board. Put on grill and turn when lightly brown. When both sides are brown place under a cotton dish towel to keep moist.

Oatmeal Mix

The best homemade, instant oatmeal mix made on the cold, winter mornings.

---

2 c quick cooking oats
½ c nonfat dry milk powder
½ c raisins
⅓ c brown sugar
1½ tsp cinnamon
¼ tsp salt
¼ tsp nutmeg

In storage container stir together all ingredients. Cover tightly and store for up to 2 months. Stir or shake before serving. Makes about 3 cups of dry mix or 6 servings.

For each serving, in microwave bowl combine ¾ c. water and ½ c. mix. Cook uncovered on 70% power for 2-3 minutes or until bubbly. Let stand for 1 minute.

White Sauce Mix

Recipe given to me from my mother-in-law and used when making creamed peas on toast and scalloped potatoes.

---

2 c instant nonfat dry milk
1 c flour
1 c butter
2 tsp salt

In large bowl combine dry milk, flour and salt. Mix well. With a pastry blender cut in butter until mixture resembles fine crumbs. Lightly pack in a large airtight container. Label White Sauce Mix and store in refrigerator. Use within 2 months. Makes about 1 quart of mix.

To MAKE basic White Sauce:

Use ½ c White Sauce Mix and 1 c cool water. Combine in a small sauce pan (for thinner sauce decrease mix to ¼ c or for thicker sauce increase mix to ¾ c). Cook over low heat until smooth, stirring constantly. Season with pepper, herbs, and spices. Makes about 1 ½ c of sauce.

Scalloped Cheesy Corn

Made on most holidays and requested by many. The cheese is what makes this dish.

2 eggs, beaten
1 (16 oz) can cream style corn
1 c shredded mozzarella cheese
1 c saltine crackers, finely crushed (28 crackers)
6 Tbsp of milk
2 Tbsp finely chopped onions
Dash of pepper
4 tsp butter

In medium bowl combine egg, corn, cheese, half of cracker crumbs, milk, onion, and pepper, mix well. Turn mixture into a well-greased baking dish. Sprinkle remaining cracker crumbs on top and dot with butter. Bake at 350 degrees about 30 minutes or until knife inserted in center comes out clean and edges of dish is nice and brown. Let stand for 5 minutes before serving.

Sweet Potato Casserole

This could be a dessert recipe, but I've traditionally made it as a side dish for Thanksgiving. Every year it is requested by our older son.

---

3 c sweet potatoes, cooked and mashed
1 c sugar
2 eggs
½ c evaporated milk
1 tsp vanilla
⅓ c butter
pinch of salt

Combine all above ingredients until smooth. Pour into 2 qt greased casserole dish. Make topping.

Topping:
⅓ c flour
1 c brown sugar
1 c flaked coconut
1 c pecans, chopped
⅓ c butter, melted

Mix all ingredients together and spread over mixture.

Bake @ 350 degrees for 35-40 minutes.

About Sue

Sue delivers encouragement through personal stories of restoration from a dark past of teenage substance abuse to discovering hope in living every day in a simple way. Her infectious, positive attitude is in every subject she speaks and writes about; from years of working in the corporate world, to personal knowledge in and around addiction, to her down to earth, honest perspective of every day life, and her journey of faith with God.

She is a survivor of a tragic motorcycle accident that propelled her into a deep relationship with God and a new view of life which is encouraging others to become all they can be. Her passion is contagious as is her down-to-earth style of writing. Once you've been around her, you leave motivated and inspired to stay positive in your own life. She walks alongside many to help them see their potential and find their own relationship with God.

For close to forty years, she has been with her husband, her Big City Boyfriend. Together they have two grown sons and one daughter-in-law, and they love to work together in gardening, on classic cars, and cooking.

Sue would love to hear from you! Stay connected and find many resources at suelhamilton.com

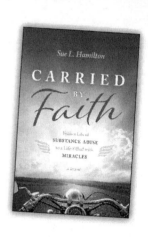
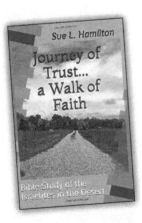